BIOTECH TRADER HANDBOOK

SECOND EDITION

THE BIOTECH TRADER HANDBOOK

A FAST, SIMPLIFIED AND EFFICIENT GUIDE TO GENERATE OUTSIZED RETURNS IN BIOTECH USING OPTIONS
(FOR THE NON-SCIENTIST)

SECOND EDITION

T. AYERS PELZ

ISBN: 1-450-59853-6
EAN-13:   9781450598538

Printed in the United States of America.

Cover design and book layout by Marni Mitchell.

ACKNOWLEDGEMENTS

To Thomas, my little office assistant and future option trader

To Bill and Lynn, your support is always appreciated

To Billy V., for getting me interested in investing

To Marni, for your design work and advice

And Most of All to My Wife Pilar, for convincing me to write this book

CONTENTS

EXHIBITS

PREFACE

Let me introduce myself. I am not a biotech expert nor do I have any background, professional or academic, in science. I basically know very little (if anything) with regards to the *science* behind drug development in the biotech industry. I am a former trader with a large, global bank's proprietary trading desk (i.e. a "prop trader") based in Europe. I was responsible for a portfolio with book limits of over $200 million. My team traded everything from futures, forex, options, credit default swaps, variance swaps, convertible bonds, straight bonds, bank loans, preferred stock, hybrids and common stock – you get the idea. I learned to trade from the institutional side (i.e. professional side). The skills I developed from this experience were invaluable.

Before prop trading, I was an M&A, corporate finance and credit banker in the U.S., Latin America, Asia and Europe for over 10 years – with regards to analyzing companies, I can tear apart the financial statements and tell you just about everything you would want to know about the financial health of a company in about an hour – stripes I earned from the continued brutal 130 hour work weeks. That's about all I will say regarding my professional background.

In 2008, I accepted a severance package from my bank. Rather than scrounge for work and publicly flog myself on LinkedIn, I decided to pursue my true passion: option trading. So I set-up a company using my hard earned savings, and started to trade options for my own account. As you may be aware, and as I quickly realized, trading for a living is a complete different lifestyle then having a salary with a big bonus at the end of year. This is an "eat what you kill" business and requires constant and aggressive diligence. I need to actively and constantly find new ways to make money on a daily basis. The specter of running out of money was (is) a constant (and terrifying) thought.

When assessing the universe of potential trading strategies to make my daily wage, I came across biotech, of which I had some prior experience trading. What has always intrigued me about biotech, especially within the volatile market that characterized 2007 ~ 2009, was its market neutral aspect – the market could be tanking and *certain* biotech stocks would either not move or they would go up. Others would get absolutely slaughtered. Those companies with near to medium term catalysts traded almost completely independent from the rest of the market.

Another, and more important aspect, especially from the perspective of an option trader, was the "defined event" aspect – drug candidate announcement dates are announced *in advance* – at times, the exact date of an announcement is given. This is different than for instance, an earnings announcement. In this case, the biotech company's entire future could be at stake. Fortunes could be made or lost in the blink of an eye, literally – hence huge price movements will, with near absolute certainty, be made. This creates a dream scenario for smart, organized and nimble option traders who are able to identify these names well in advance. Even when one arrives late to the event (i.e. a FDA or clinical trial catalyst event), with the versatility afforded by using options, there are other styles of trades one can execute to profit handsomely. I became very excited – I immediately knew this would generate some decent upside and become a core element, amongst many elements, of my overall trading strategy.

So I naively set about to study every possible aspect of "biotech." I read books (most published more than 10 years ago and therefore of limited use) and articles on the internet, I studied university textbooks, read magazines, etc. I even considered taking biochemistry classes at a local university. After several weeks of intense study, I realized and accepted that I would never be able to understand the underlying science of each company's drug candidate(s). I know now, however, that having this specific, deep knowledge is actually not necessary (although it would be nice). Drug trials are tricky – even with a PhD in the underlying science, an outsider will <u>never</u> know, with certainty, if the FDA decision or clinical trial will turn out to be positive or negative given all of the variables involved (if one could, they would be the richest person alive). If someone tells you or claims their knowledge in the subject qualifies them to more accurately assess the outcome of a catalyst event, they are lying or self-delusional. Perhaps they will understand the *results* once announced as being negative or positive but this is irrelevant as the market will immediately assess the value for you post-announcement (as evidenced by the movement in the share price). Perhaps they will argue, for example, that they can better assess the structure of a trial (and therefore the likelihood for positive or negative results) – even then, they still cannot ascertain whether or not the trial will be successful. Forget about it – as far as I am concerned, the playing field is flat with regards to this element. I realized this presented a huge opportunity.

With this in mind, over the next six months, I developed and honed a fast, simplified and efficient process to assess opportunity in biotech. Using this streamlined construct, my goal was to assess **every** listed biotech company meeting specific criteria as fast as possible. Yes, that meant hundreds of companies – I didn't care. Following the assessment, I would either initiate a trade or not. That was the plan.

My hard work paid off. In the first six months, I generated hundreds of thousands of dollars in profits trading both successful *and* unsuccessful FDA and clinical trial catalysts. This may not seem like much, but in order to generate these returns, I risked less than $25,000 in total. Yeah, that's right, less than $25,000. I could have potentially generated over $1,000,000 but I value risk-adjusted returns over straight out gambling that I (and you should) refuse to do. I made this money using "smart," opportunity-specific strategies: leveraged calls (risk reversals), combinations of Puts and Calls (short and long), vertical spreads, butterflies, hedged short straddles/strangles, playing the explosion/collapse in volatility, extreme (i.e. + 350%) high volatility strategies, you name it – every opportunity and associated trade structure played off of the individual strengths and weaknesses of the company *and* the situation.

This book's main purpose is to provide individuals with some knowledge of options a simple and efficient way to get involved in the world of biotech *as fast as possible*. Using my techniques and methodologies, any reader of this book who understands options, with the proper analysis and trade construct, in addition to a good sense of work ethic, can potentially achieve solid results. I obviously cannot guarantee that you will profit from this knowledge, nor should you infer otherwise, but using these strategies and techniques may accelerate your ability to actively trade, in a knowledgeable manner, in these situations.

Good luck to you.

Tony Pelz

Denver, January 2011

"...THIS IS THE LESSON. NEVER GIVE IN. NEVER, NEVER, NEVER, NEVER — IN NOTHING, GREAT OR SMALL, LARGE OR PETTY — NEVER GIVE IN..."

WINSTON CHURCHILL
OCTOBER 29, 1941

PART I

CHAPTER 1.0

BACKGROUND

1.1 THE FDA CLINICAL TRIAL PROCESS

Overview

First off, it is essential to gain a basic understanding of the drug development process within the context of the Food and Drug Administration ("FDA") clinical trial structure as it provides the basis for the entire trading strategy presented in this book.

In order to bring a drug candidate from concept to an approved and marketed drug, a sponsoring company needs to move the drug candidate through a series of "trials," coordinating with and seeking approval from the FDA at nearly each step. These trials are broadly divided into three phases (after Pre-Clinical studies). There is no need for fifty pages on this subject – the essential elements of each step of the overall drug development process are ordered numerically and listed below[1]:

---

[1] Source: Adapted from information contained on Clinicaltrials.gov.

(1) Pre-Clinical

The Pre-Clinical phase involves researching and testing new drug candidates in the laboratory and on animals. The primary goal of the Pre-Clinical phase, amongst others, is to determine if the identified drug candidate is safe on humans. The Pre-Clinical phase can take from 3 to 5 years (and possibly longer) to complete.

(2) File IND with FDA

Drug candidates that show very promising results in Pre-Clinical studies may be moved to Phase I by filing an IND ("Investigational New Drug Application") with the FDA and receiving their approval. An IND essentially seeks FDA approval to allow the company to initiate the testing of the drug on humans. The IND also, amongst other elements, includes detailed information on the structure of the trials the company intends to use for testing the drug.

(3) Phase I

In Phase I trials, researchers test the experimental drug candidate in a small group of people (20 - 80) for the first time **to evaluate its safety**, determine a safe dosage range, and identify side effects. Phase I can take up to 1 year. There is no guarantee the experimental drug or treatment will move to Phase II.

(4) Phase II

Assuming positive results are achieved in Phase I, the drug candidate may move to Phase II. In Phase II trials, the experimental drug candidate is given to a larger group of people (100 - 300) to see if it **is effective (efficacy) and to further evaluate its safety**. Phase II can take from 1 to 2 years. The company must seek FDA approval to proceed to Phase III. Following a successful Phase II, a company often, although not always, seeks a Special Protocol Assessment ("SPA") from the FDA. This is a declaration by the FDA that the up-and-coming Phase III trial's design, clinical endpoints and other trial elements, if met, will be acceptable for an FDA approval. This may enhance the likelihood of FDA approval upon successful Phase III data.

(5) Phase III

In Phase III trials, the experimental drug candidate is given to large groups of people (1,000 - 3,000) to **confirm its effectiveness, monitor side effects, compare it to commonly used treatments, and collect information that will allow the experimental drug or treatment to be used safely**. Phase III can take from 1 – 4 years. The company will file an NDA ("New Drug Application" or BLA, "Biologics License Application"[2]) with the FDA with positive Phase III results.

(6) File NDA with FDA

Prior to marketing the drug candidate, the company must file an NDA with the FDA. This proposal seeks to gain the FDA's approval of the new drug for sale in the U.S. The application must provide sufficient evidence for the FDA to decide that the drug is safe and effective and that all other FDA criteria are met. Applications often run hundreds of thousands of pages long and include all information from not only every clinical trial but also pre-clinical data. It should be noted at this juncture that a positive Phase III does not guarantee an ultimate approval of the drug candidate – the FDA first needs to review all data. The FDA has 60 days to accept the NDA or reject it (due to it being incomplete). If the NDA is rejected the company will rectify the deficiencies and resubmit.

---

[2] The BLA is equivalent to the NDA for a "Biologic."

(7) FDA Review

It can take around 1 to 2 years for the FDA to fully review an NDA. You will often see references to a PDUFA date. PDUFA ("The Prescription Drug User Fee Act")[3] was created to help shorten the lengthy NDA review time. The act allows the FDA to collect user fees from pharmaceutical companies in order to expedite the review. The act specifies that the FDA review drug applications from six to twelve months depending upon the nature of the drug. For example, a drug candidate that targets a disease where there is currently no treatment will have a higher priority than a drug with many competing treatments.

The PDUFA date is the approximate date when the FDA will render a decision with regards to the NDA.[4] During the review, the FDA assesses the drug candidate's safety and effectiveness. The FDA also reviews the proposed labeling for the drug and inspects the facilities where the drug is to be manufactured. During the review process, the FDA may also convene an "Advisory Panel" (or Advisory Committee) to further review the drug candidate. An Advisory Panel is a single day meeting where independent industry experts review and opine on a drug candidate's data presented by the company and FDA reviewers. At the end of the meeting a vote is taken by the committee to decide whether or not to approve the drug and under what conditions, if any. A positive committee vote normally bodes very well for the company's drug candidate whereas a negative vote can be quite damaging for the drug candidate's prospects. It is important to note that the FDA is not required to follow the recommendations of the Committee (but usually does). Advisory Panels present interesting trading opportunities – this will be discussed in Section 5.17.

---

[3] Pronounced "padoofa" in the industry.

[4] The FDA response is on or around the PDUFA date. In some situations, the FDA may reschedule or delay a PDUFA date by a few weeks to a few months.

5

Once the FDA's review is complete, the NDA will be approved or rejected. If the drug candidate is rejected, the FDA issues a "Complete Response Letter" or CRL, which provides the sponsoring company a rationale for the rejection and what data, if any, could be provided to make the application acceptable. Often, the FDA may require additional trials – this can take several additional years and can be devastating to the company. The FDA often makes a tentative approval requesting that a minor deficiency or other issue be corrected before an approval is granted. If the drug candidate is approved, the company can then bring the drug to market.

Conclusion

The key point to understand about the trial construct is that **the drug development process can take well over 10 years before it produces a marketable drug that can generate revenues for the sponsoring company**. During the entire process, the developing company will invest significant financial resources, which it may or may not have or may need to raise, to move each candidate through each phase. It has been estimated that moving a drug from discovery, through each trial phase and ultimately to the market costs well over $800 million.[5] At each phase, the probability of failure is extremely high. For every 5,000 to 10,000 compounds that enter pre-clinical testing, one is approved for marketing.[6] A failed drug candidate can prove fatal to an emerging biotech company.

---

[5] DiMassi J. "The value of improving the productivity of the drug development process: faster times and better decisions". Pharmacoeconomics 20 Suppl 3:1-10. DiMassi J., Hansen R., Grabowski H (2003). "The price of innovation: new estimate of drug development costs." J Health Econ 22 (2): 151:85.

[6] Klees JE, Joines R. Occupational health issues in pharmaceutical research and development process. Occupational Medicine 1997; 12:5-27.

1.2 TRADING THESIS & BOOK FOCUS

The primary focus of this book, and the basis for the trading strategies described herein, is to focus on (a) small cap biotech companies (b) with one or more Phase III drug candidate(s) *where result announcements or catalyst events are due under a year and a half*[7] and (c) where the company has listed options. These three elements combined create unusual catalyst events that contribute to spectacular trading opportunities with near absolute certainty.

Companies with Phase III Candidates

First of all, as described above, Phase III clinical trial and FDA related events are the ultimate stock moving catalysts, either negative or positive, for the **small cap** biotech company. In this case, and depending upon each individual company's situation, the impact on the share price can and usually will be substantial – as traders, this is exactly where we want to be.

Focusing on companies whose leading drug candidate is in Phase I or Phase II *normally* lacks this key catalyst event. If you are an "investor," and you buy the common stock (or worse, the options) of one of these companies (Phase I/II), then fine – just realize you will be holding the shares for well over 5 years, at least, you will get no dividends, your company will likely continue to face financial challenges as you face multiple dilutive events as the company raises funds to continue trials (oh, and by the way, the out of the money options you purchased will likely turn out to be worthless). At the end of the line, the entire company could go bankrupt on a failed clinical trial or FDA event. Your

---

[7] When I refer to "Phase III catalyst events" throughout the book, I am including both clinical trial and catalyst events that follow during the FDA review process such as Advisory Panels or PDUFA dates, amongst others.

patience will have been for naught.[8] Focusing on a company with a Phase III event within under a year and half, will allow you to fast forward to the ultimate catalyst event.

Companies with Options

Where possible, your focus should be on companies where you can trade options. Obviously this is not possible on most developing small cap biotech companies, but your focus should be on these companies, nevertheless. The (obvious) rational is that there is more flexibility with regards to the trade structure. When only the common stock can be traded, you can either buy or, where possible, short. With options, the trade structure can be tailored to fit the event and is virtually unlimited. In addition, the trade structure can be adjusted during the trade to fit new issues which eventually come up over the period of the trade. In the chapter on Trade Structures, we will review these strategies in detail.

Structure of this Book

This book is structured into six key chapters:

Trade Candidate Identification: This chapter quickly reviews how to find small cap biotech companies, provides a list of biotech related internet resources, lists small cap biotech tickers and provides some advice on developing a company database.

Trade Candidate Analysis: This chapter provides a structured, simplified and efficient approach to analyzing small cap biotech companies as fast as possible. The review process covers analysis of small cap biotech company cash profile,

---

[8] Although Phase III opportunities are the primary focus of this book, strategies targeting Phase I and Phase II opportunities will be quickly covered later in the book.

ownership structure, insider activity, analysts views, technical analysis, pipeline and industry support.

Option Basics: This chapter reviews options from a *trading perspective*. The primary goal is to provide the reader a conceptual understanding of how options work and how they can be used to make money.

Trading Strategy & Tactics: This chapter covers several trading techniques, strategies and tactics when trading both illiquid option markets and small cap biotech companies.

Trade Structures: This chapter details selected trading structures appropriate for small cap biotech. This chapter also reviews notes regarding trading companies with only Phase I and II candidates and discusses trading structures that are not recommended.

Trade Process: This chapter describers a process to follow when there is no initial bullish, bearish or neutral trade conviction (as is often the situation when trading FDA and clinical trial catalysts). Several trade examples are provided at the end of the chapter.

CHAPTER 2.0

TRADE CANDIDATE IDENTIFICATION

2.1 OVERVIEW

The first step in the trade process is the identification of a good universe of trade candidates. This process can be approached passively (where specific ideas are generated from external sources) or actively (where you do your own research to generate trade ideas). Whatever approach you eventually use, this section seeks to provide the essential tools and structure that will make this process as efficient as possible.

2.2 SMALL CAP BIOTECH TRADER TOOLS

2.2.1 FDA & Clinical Trial Calendar

One of the most useful tools for identifying trades in small cap biotech is a good FDA and clinical trial calendar. This calendar lists the exact or approximate date of small cap biotech catalysts. A good calendar will contain the dates of FDA Advisory Panels (including briefing document release dates), PDUFA dates, NDA related filing time estimates, (approximate) Phase 1/2/3 status/data releases and other FDA and company related actions. Putting together an FDA and clinical trial calendar is *extremely* tedious and time consuming (it requires reading press releases, corporate presentations and FDA/pipeline information for each individual drug candidate of every listed small cap biotech stock!).

Luckily, there are very good on-line resources that have done the work for you –
a select few are listed in Exhibit 2.1.

Exhibit 2.1: FDA & Clinical Trial Calendar On-line Resources

Name	Web Address
BioPharm Catalyst	www.biopharmcatalyst.com
BioRunUp (subscription based)	www.biorunup.com
GekkoWire	www.gekkowire.com
The Biotech Investment Paradigm	www.biotechinvestmentparadigm.com

It is important to note that all FDA and clinical trial related data should be
double checked prior to executing a trade as information contained in on-line
resources can potentially be out-of-date – Section 3.7: Pipeline covers how to
verify this type of data.

2.2.2 Twitter Account

It may surprise you but Twitter is an excellent trading tool (I was initially
skeptical of this resource). Twitter allows the user to "follow" active traders,
investors, bloggers, analysts and other industry professionals and participants *in
real-time*. Following the Twitter feeds of active users is excellent for trade
candidate identification, company specific news and research amongst other
uses. Twitter allows one to see what these people are doing and thinking. Most
traders or industry professionals with a large "following" also have their own
blogs that often detail their trade ideas and/or company research which can be
very valuable when assessing opportunities.

Information "tweeted"[9] on Twitter can often be of high tactical value. News
related items tend to (always) hit Twitter faster than major media outlets such as
Yahoo! Finance or CNBC – this is because the people you are following often

---

[9] A "Tweet" is a 140-character message posted on Twitter.

have access to news sources you do not or the news is on a smaller company (most small cap biotech) that does not warrant mainstream coverage. This near "instantaneous" news feature via Twitter is extremely valuable in a live trading situation. For example, I was on vacation and was long Chelsea Therapeutics (Ticker: CHTP) 5.0 strike Calls that were set to expire worthless with about 20 minutes left to trade on a Friday (the stock was around $4.50). Data on one of Chelsea's Phase 3 drug candidates was slated to be released *at any moment*. The stock proceeded to immediately spike up to around $6 – there was no news and I had no other information. Did the company release data? What was going on? I checked Yahoo! Finance and the company's website – nothing. I checked Twitter and I read that someone was on CNBC pumping the stock – this was not Phase 3 data related: I immediately closed out my Calls at a substantial profit with around 10 minutes left to trade. The shares closed at around $5 at the end of the day (the Calls would have expired nearly worthless) – without Twitter, I would have been "flying blind" and most likely would have missed the opportunity. If you actively trade small cap biotech, Twitter is a must have and must use tool in your daily trading arsenal.

In order to use Twitter, first set up an account (at www.twitter.com) and then begin to "follow" people. To start following small cap biotech related feeds, you may want to initially follow me: **biotechtraderHB**. Once you follow me, you can see whom I follow and add those individuals if they pique your interest. Prior to following someone it is often useful to see what kind of information they tweet – this can be accomplished by reading their prior tweets (click on the "tweets" link under their name). If the information seems useful, you can choose to "follow" them.

2.2.3 On-line resources

There are some extremely good on-line resources for small cap biotech traders and investors. Exhibit 2.2 provides a select few on-line resources that I view as currently amongst the best. It is important to note that while General News and FDA-related sites are good[10] most of the value-added research and trade related ideas are found on the Blogs and Full Coverage sites.

Exhibit 2.2: Websites for Biotech Traders

GENERAL NEWS:	**OFFICIAL TRIAL DATA:**
www.biospace.com	www.clinicaltrials.gov
www.clinicaspace.com	www.fda.gov
www.fiercebiotech.com	
www.finance.yahoo.com	**BLOGS:**
www.thestreet.com	www.biotechtraderhandbook.com
	www.seekingalpha.com
FULL COVERAGE:	
www.biorunup.com (subscription)	**OTHER SOCIAL MEDIA:**
www.biotechinvestmentparadigm.com	www.stocktwits.com
www.biopharmcatalyst.com	
www.biomedreports.com	**OTHER:**
www.gekkowire.com	www.bigcharts.com
	www.nasdaqtrader.com*
INSIDER ACTIVITY:	www.shortsqueeze.com
www.mffais.com (subscription)	www.tickerspy.com
www.secform4.com	

Primarily for after-hours trades and trading halt information.

---

[10] Be warned: the FDA sites may be a bit arcane and confusing to those new to trial related catalyst trading. Most of the high level data needed to make an educated trade can be found either in company press releases, blogs or full coverage sites.

2.3 COMPREHENSIVE INDUSTRY SEARCH

2.3.1 Overview

While most on-line resources are useful to identify trade candidates, they tend to cover companies and opportunities everyone else is evaluating *at the same time* – this can place you at a significant disadvantage. For this reason, it is often advantageous to employ a comprehensive industry search approach to identify trade candidates well before everyone else. Although *significantly* more tedious and time consuming, this approach often yields substantial opportunities to generate outsized returns.

2.3.2 Trade Candidate Ticker List

The first part of this approach is to generate a ticker list. The best way to do this is to use a stock screening tool on either a brokerage website or free web service (such as Yahoo! Finance). A high quality and comprehensive list can be generated by searching under two broad parameters: industry and stock price range. For industry, search under biotechnology, small cap biotech, pharmaceuticals or other healthcare related terms. For stock price range, I suggest a range of $0.50 to $10 or $20 – this will generally produce a high quality list of trade candidates with market capitalizations[11] under $500 million. I avoid stocks with prices below $0.50 because the output is usually hundreds of stocks with prices of a few pennies to $0.10 that are generally not worth the time and effort to do follow-up research either because they lack sufficient liquidity, are too early stage, face severe financial distress or any other number of problematic issues.

Exhibit 2.3 lists the identified small cap biotech trade candidates using this approach. I include the company name, the ticker and the company website. As

---

[11] Market Capitalization ("market cap.") = stock price x common shares outstanding.

the data in Exhibit 2.3 will change substantially over time, it is highly recommend to eventually perform your own search to generate an up-to-date ticker list.

Exhibit 2.3: Trade Candidate Ticker List

Ticker	Company	Website
ABIO	ARCA Biopharma	Arcadiscovery.com
ACAD	Acadia Pharmaceuticals	Acadia-pharm.com
ACHN	Achillion Pharmaceuticals	Achillion.com
ACOR	Acorda Therapeutics	Acorda.com
ADLR	Adolor	Adolor.com
AEZS	Aeterna Zentaris	Aezsinc.com
AGEN	Antigenics	Antigenics.com
ALKS	Alkermes	Alkermes.com
ALNY	Alnylam Pharmaceuticals	Alnylam.com
ALTH	Allos Therapeutics	Allos.com
ALTU	Altus Pharmaceuticals	Altus.com
ALXA	Alexza Pharmaceuticals	Alexza.com
AMRI	Albany Molecular Research	Amriglobal.com
AMRN	Amarin	Amarincorp.com
ANDS	Anadys	Anadyspharma.com
ANIK	Anika Therapeutics	Anikatherapeutics.com
ANPI	Angiotech Pharmaceuticals	Angiotech.com
ANX	ADVENTRX Pharma	Adventrx.com
APPY	AspenBio Pharma	Aspenbiopharma.com
ARIA	Ariad Pharmaceuticals	Ariad.com
ARNA	Arena Pharmaceuticals	Arenapharm.com
ARQL	ArQule	Arqule.com
ARRY	Array BioPharma	Arraybiopharma.com
ATHX	Athersys Inc.	Athersys.com
AVII	AVI BioPharma	Avibio.com

Exhibit 2.3: Trade Candidate Ticker List (Continued)

Ticker	Company	Website
AVNR	Avanir Pharmaceuticals	Avanir.com
BCRX	BioCryst Pharmaceuticals	Biocryst.com
BDSI	BioDelivery Sciences Int'l	Bdsinternational.com
BIOD	Biodel Inc.	Biodel.com
BMRN	BioMarin Pharmaceuticals	Bmrn.com
BPAX	BioSante Pharmaceuticals	Biosantepharma.com
CADX	Cadence Pharmaceuticals	Cadencepharm.com
CBLI	Cleveland BioLabs	Cbiolabs.com
CBM	Cambrex Corp.	Cambrex.com
CBRX	Columbia Laboratories, Inc.	Columbialabs.com
CBST	Cubist	Cubist.com
CERS	Cerus Corp.	Cerus.com
CGEN	Compugen Ltd.	Cgen.com
CHTP	Chelsea Therapeutics	Chelseatherapeutics.com
CLDA	Clinical Data	Clda.com
CLDX	Celldex Therapeutics	Celldextherapeutics.com
CLSN	Celsion Corp.	Celsion.com
CORT	Corcept Therapeutics	Corcept.com
CRIS	Curis Inc.	Curis.com
CRME	Cardiome Pharma	Cardiome.com
CRXX	CombinatoRx	Combinatorx.com
CRY	CryoLife Inc.	Cryolife.com
CTIC	Cell Therapeutics	Celltherapeutics.com
CYTK	Cytokinetics	Cytokinetics.com
CYTX	Cytori Therapeutics	Cytoritx.com
DCTH	Delcath Systems	Delcath.com
DEPO	Depomed	Depomedinc.com
DRRX	Durect	Durect.com
DSCO	Discovery Labs	Discoverylabs.com

Exhibit 2.3: Trade Candidate Ticker List (Continued)

Ticker	Company	Website
DVAX	Dynavax Technologies	Dynavax.com
DYAX	Dyax Corp.	Dayax.com
EBS	Emergent BioSolutions	Emergentbiosolutions.com
ENMD	EntreMed, Inc.	Entremed.com
ENZ	Enzo	Enzo.com
EXAS	Exact Sciences Corp.	Exactsciences.com
EXEL	Exelixis	Exelixis.com
FACT	Facet Biotech	Facetbiotech.com
FOLD	Amicus Therapeutics	Amicustherapeutics.com
GERN	Geron	Geron.com
GNVC	GenVec, Inc.	Genvec.com
GTXI	GTx Inc.	Gtxinc.com
HALO	Halozyme Therapeutics	Halozyme.com
HEB	Hemispherx Biopharma	Hemispherx.net
HEPH	Hollis-Eden Pharmaceuticals	Holliseden.com
ICGN	ICAgen Inc.	Icagen.com
IDIX	Idenix	Idenix.com
INCY	Incyte	Incite.com
INFI	Infinity Pharmaceuticals	Ipi.com
INHX	Inhibitex	Inhibitex.com
IMGN	ImmunoGen	Immunogen.com
IMMU	Immunomedics	Immunomedics.com
ISIS	Isis Pharmaceuticals	Isispharm.com
ISPH	Inspire Pharmaceuticals	Inspirepharm.com
ISTA	ISTA Pharmaceuticals	Istavision.com
ITMN	Intermune	Intermune.com
JAZZ	JAZZ Pharmaceuticals	Jazzpharmaceuticals.com
KERX	Keryx Biopharmaceuticals	Keryx.com
KOOL	ThermoGenesis Corp.	Thermogenesis.com

17

Exhibit 2.3: Trade Candidate Ticker List (Continued)

Ticker	Company	Website
LGND	Ligand Pharmaceuticals	Ligand.com
MAPP	MAP Pharmaceuticals	Mappharma.com
MAXY	Maxygen	Maxygen.com
MBRK	Middlebrook Pharma	Middlebrookpharma.com
MDCO	The Medicines Company	Themedicinescompany.com
MITI	Micromet	Micromet-inc.com
MNKD	MannKind Corporation	Mannkindcorp.com
MNTA	Momenta Pharmaceuticals	Momentapharma.com
MSHL	Marshall Edwards	Marshalledwardsinc.com
MYRX	Myriad Pharmaceuticals	Myriadpharma.com
NABI	Nabi Pharmaceuticals	Nabi.com
NBIX	Neurocrine Biosciences	Neurocrine.com
NBY	NovaBay Pharmaceuticals	Novabaypharma.com
NEOL	NeoPharm, Inc.	Neopharm.com
NKTR	Nektar	Nectar.com
NPSP	NPS Pharmaceuticals	Npsp.com
NVAX	Novavax	Novavax.com
NVGN	Novogen	Novogen.com
NYMX	Nymox Pharmaceutical Inc.	Nymox.com
OMER	Omeros Corp.	Omeros.com
ONCY	Oncolytics Biotech Inc.	Oncolyticsbiotech.com
ONTY	Oncothyreon Inc.	Oncothyreon.com
OPTR	Optimer Pharmaceuticals	Optimerpharma.com
OPXA	Opexa Therapeutics	Opexatherapeutics.com
OREX	Orexigen	Orexigen.com
OSIR	Osiris Therapeutics	Osiristx.com
OSUR	OrasSure Technologies	Orasure.com
OXGN	OXiGENE	Oxigene.com
PARD	Poniard Pharmaceuticals	Poniard.com

Exhibit 2.3: Trade Candidate Ticker List (Continued)

Ticker	Company	Website
PCYC	Pharmacyclics	Pharmacyclics.com
PDLI	PDL BioPharma	Pdl.com
PGNX	Progenics Pharmaceuticals	Progenics.com
PLX	Protalix Biotherapeutics	Protalix.com
POZN	Pozen Pharmaceuticals	Pozen.com
PPCO	Penwest	Penw.com
PPHM	Peregrine Pharmaceuticals	Peregrineinc.com
PSDV	pSivida Corp.	Psivida.com
PTIE	Pain Therapeutics	Paintrials.com
QLTI	QLT, Inc.	Qltinc.com
REGN	Regeneron Pharmaceuticals	Regeneron.com
RGN	Regenerx	Regenerx.com
RIGL	Rigel Pharmaceuticals	Rigel.com
RMTI	Rockwell Medical	Rockwellmed.com
RPRX	Repros Therapeutics	Reprosrx.com
SCLN	SciClone Pharmaceuticals	Sciclone.com
SCMP	Sucampo Parmaceuticals	Sucampo.com
SGEN	SeattleGenetics	Seagen.com
SGMO	Sangamo BioSciences	Sangamo.com
SIGA	SIGA	Siga.com
SNSS	Sunesis Pharmaceuticals	Sunesis-pharma.com
SNTA	Synta Pharmaceuticals	Syntapharma.com
SPPI	Spectrum Pharmaceuticals	Spectrumpharm.com
STEM	StemCells	Stemcellsinc.com
SVNT	Savient Pharmaceuticals	Savientpharma.com
SUPG	SuperGen	Supergen.com
TELK	Telik, Inc.	Telik.com
THLD	Threshold Pharmaceuticals	Thresholdpharm.com
THRX	Theravance	Theravance.com

Exhibit 2.3: Trade Candidate Ticker List (Continued)

Ticker	Company	Website
TRMS	Trimeris	Trimeris.com
VICL	Vical	Vical.com
VNDA	Vanda Pharmaceuticals	Vandapharmaceuticals.com
VPHM	Viropharma Incorporated	Viropharma.com
VVUS	Vivus	Vivus.com
XNPT	XenoPort	Xenopart.com
XOMA	XOMA	Xoma.com
YMI	YM Biosciences	Ymbiosciences.com
ZGEN	ZymoGenetics	Zymogenetics.com
ZIOP	ZIOPHARM Oncology	Ziopharm.com

2.3.3 Organization Strategy

Once you generate a ticker list, the tedious and time consuming part begins (for the highly motivated person): the individual analysis of the component stocks in the ticker list. A streamlined approach to performing this analysis on each company will be covered in Chapter 3.0: Trade Candidate Analysis.[12] Prior to this, however, it is essential to put in place the infrastructure to properly organize your analysis (as you will eventually analyze hundreds of companies). The more organized you are, the more success you will have trading small cap biotech – this is a certainty.

No matter how thorough you intend to be, a simple yet highly effective approach is to buy a (large) three ring binder notebook and A-Z letter tabs. For each company your come across, use a single sheet of paper to write your notes (i.e. key dates, critical financial data, analyst estimates, etc.) – it helps to write the company's ticker on the upper right hand corner of the sheet for easy reference.

---

[12] Of course, this analysis construct can and should be applied to trade candidates sourced passively, i.e. from blogs, full coverage sites or FDA and clinical trial calendars.

For each individual company sheet, include a print out of the company's pipeline chart. Once you are finished, file the sheet alphabetically based on the company's ticker in the notebook.

After looking at few hundred companies you will have a sizeable database (mine is a binder notebook nearly 3 inches thick) of information that you can go back to (frequently) and quickly review if necessary. If you don't do this, you will find yourself getting confused given the vast number of companies; if you do what I say regarding organization, you will find that having the information at hand (immediately) will save you substantial time and better position you to jump on emerging opportunities (which will, without a doubt, come up). For example, biotech company XYZ just dropped 30%. You recognize said company, and quickly access your notes on the company. You see a trade and feel comfortable putting the trade on *immediately* (because you know the key elements / key drivers of the company as per your notes). If you are stumbling around, you will miss the opportunity – don't let it happen to you; it will cost you dearly over time.

For Phase I/II companies, simply write the phase of the primary drug candidate in addition to the expected date of review, if any (or additional information if you wish) – this will allow you to build a pipeline list of trade candidates *well in advance* and give you a huge edge in building your trade positions prior to others (the "day trading hoard") discovering the company. This will increase the probability of generating huge returns in the future. Believe me on that.

CHAPTER 3.0

TRADE CANDIDATE ANALYSIS

3.1 FAST REVIEW STRUCTURE OVERVIEW

In order to analyze identified trade candidates, an efficient review methodology must be utilized. In Exhibit 3.1 I present a seven step, streamlined review structure, which I aptly call Fast Review Structure ("FRS"). This review structure has been developed in order to achieve a simple yet extensive analysis *as fast as possible*. The goal of FRS is to quickly determine if there is a potential, high risk-adjusted return trade and if so, what type of approach (i.e. bearish, bullish, neutral) and trade structure to use. The structure should be used to identify a core list of companies where high potential trades can be made and provide a springboard for further, more in-depth analysis prior to an eventual trade, if necessary.

Exhibit 3.1: Fast Review Structure Components

Cash Profile	Technical Analysis
Ownership	Pipeline
Insider Activity	Industry Support
Analyst Views	

3.2 CASH PROFILE

3.2.1 Overview

The fastest and most efficient way to analyze the financial position of a small cap biotech company is to focus primarily on its cash profile. This analysis looks at cash burn, cash per share, net cash/net debt balances and future sources of cash. This information alone will tell you about all you need to know regarding the financial health of the company.

The first place you should check for this information is the company's latest earnings press release. The earnings release will normally include a quick overview of the company's cash profile often including cash burn estimates and any planned information about future cash sources. Other components of the company's cash profile, such as cash per share and net cash/net debt balances can be easily calculated with information contained in this release. If you need access to more detailed information, check inside the SEC 10-Q (quarterly report) or 10-K (annual report).

For example, ACADIA Pharmaceutical's (Ticker: ACAD) 2Q'09 earnings press release, located in SEC Form 8-K, contained most all of the information needed to quickly get a handle on the company's cash profile. The most important information from this perspective is contained in paragraphs three and nine shown in Exhibit 3.2.

Paragraph 3:

"At June 30, 2009, ACADIA's cash, cash equivalents, and investment securities totaled $60.1 million at December 31, 2008. The increase in cash was primarily due to an upfront cash payment of $30 million received in May 2009 pursuant to ACADIA's collaboration with Biovail, partially offset by cash used to fund operations."

Paragraph 9:

"ACADIA continues to anticipate that its cash, cash equivalents and investment securities will be greater than $40 million at December 31, 2009, and that the Company's existing cash resources and payments from its collaborations will be sufficient to fund its operations at least into the first half of 2011."

Source: SEC Form 8-K.

In these two paragraphs, it is revealed how much cash the company has and how long the company expects to survive without raising external funds (i.e. its cash burn). The information needed to calculate cash per share (cash, shares outstanding), net cash/net debt balances (cash, debt) and future sources of cash (milestone and collaborative revenues, existing product revenues) are located further in the release.

3.2.2 Cash Burn

Cash burn is one of the key data points in the analysis of a small cap biotech company. It provides a financial timeline to look into the future, identifying when and at what levels future cash balances intersect with key dates (i.e. FDA and clinical trial announcements, debt maturity dates, milestone achievement dates, etc.) thus providing a trader a more informed rationale to both plan and structure trades. It is essential to know this information.

Exhibit 3.3: ACADIA 2Q'09 Financials

ACADIA PHARMACEUTICALS INC.
CONDENSED CONSOLIDATED STATEMENTS OF OPERATIONS
(in thousands, except per share amounts)
(Unaudited)

	Three Months Ended June 30,		Six Months Ended June 30,	
	2009	2008	2009	2008
Collaborative revenues	$ 1,820	$ 177	$ 2,194	$ 983
Operating expenses				
Research and development (includes stock-based compensation of $283, $380, $504 and $795, respectively)	11,979	16,036	24,533	31,207
General and administrative (includes stock-based compensation of $333, $431, $687 and $852, respectively)	2,662	3,184	5,649	6,454
Total operating expenses	14,641	19,220	30,182	37,661
Loss from operations	(12,821)	(19,043)	(27,988)	(36,678)
Interest income (expense), net	93	756	260	2,011
Net loss	$(12,728)	$(18,287)	$(27,728)	$(34,667)
Net loss per common share, basic and diluted	$ (0.34)	$ (0.49)	$ (0.75)	$ (0.94)
Weighted average common shares outstanding, basic and diluted	37,220	37,102	37,200	37,077

ACADIA PHARMACEUTICALS INC.
CONDENSED CONSOLIDATED BALANCE SHEETS
(in thousands)
(Unaudited)

	June 30, 2009	December 31, 2008(1)
Assets		
Cash, cash equivalents, and investment securities	$ 66,152	$ 60,083
Prepaid expenses, receivables and other current assets	2,062	2,299
Total current assets	68,214	62,382
Property and equipment, net	1,657	2,103
Other assets	192	192
Total assets	$ 70,063	$ 64,677
Liabilities and Stockholders' Equity		
Current liabilities	20,936	11,051
Long-term liabilities	22,714	634
Stockholders' equity	26,413	52,992
Total liabilities and stockholders' equity	$ 70,063	$ 64,677

(1) The condensed consolidated balance sheet at December 31, 2008 has been derived from the audited financial statements at that date but does not include all of the information and footnotes required by accounting principles generally accepted in the United States for complete financial statements.

Source: SEC Form 8-K.

Occasionally, companies will not include explicit cash burn calculations in their press release. Under such a scenario, you will need to estimate the cash burn amount yourself. A "quick and dirty" way to estimate cash burn is to use the simple formula below (for quarterly data):

= Total Cash / [(R&D + SG&A + other operating expenses - non-recurring expenses +/- net interest expense – total revenue (either from products, license fees, or milestone/collaboration amounts or other revenue amounts)][13 = Number of Quarters of Cash Remaining

For example, using the information contained in ACADIA's Statement of Operations, in Exhibit 3.3, we get:

$$= 66,152 / [(11,979 + 2,662 + 0 - 0 - 93 - 1,820)] = 5.2 \text{ Quarters}$$

ACADIA states, as of June 30, 2009, that the company will have sufficient cash to fund operations at least into the first half of 2011 (or approximately 6 quarters) – excluding any external capital raising efforts. As you can see, our quick and dirty calculation of 5.2 quarters is not far off. When doing this type of analysis, make sure to exclude expense and/or revenue amounts that are not expected to re-occur going forward. For example, if the company discontinued research or a trial on a potential drug candidate, your forward looking and on-going operating expense estimate may be too high and will thus need to be adjusted – if this amount is material, the company will usually mention it in their press release – make a note of it and adjust accordingly. With regards to milestone payments or other collaborative revenues be aware that these are awarded only after meeting certain criteria. For this reason, it is important to always analyze the component parts of a company's cash burn estimates. It is a good idea to only include funds (perhaps as a scenario) that have been received or are going to be received with absolute certainty. The company may say that they expect to receive uncertain milestone funds, but this is not guaranteed – take notice of this eventuality on your cash burn calculations.

---

[13] Other recurring cash items such as income tax, capex, loan amortization amongst other similar items, should be added into this equation where information is available/applicable. Small cap biotech financials are usually quite simple and these additional adjustments, however, are usually not necessary in order to get a general idea regarding cash burn.

3.2.3 Cash per Share

Another useful way to look at cash when analyzing small cap biotech is from the perspective of cash per share. This is obviously calculated by taking total cash (less debt, if any) and dividing by total (diluted) shares outstanding. The cash per share metric is useful from a variety of perspectives. First, it can provide a flash estimate of where the market is valuing a company's drug candidate(s). For example, Pain Therapeutics (Ticker: PTIE) as of 3Q'09 had total shares outstanding of 42.2 million and total cash and marketable securities of $177.5 equating to cash per share of $4.21 (the company has no debt). This compared to a market share price of $4.90. This implies that the market views the total value of future products at around $0.70 a share (or $29.5 million) that may or may not be correct. Second, the metric can indicate potentially irrational situations where cash per share exceeds price per share (i.e. the current market price). For example, small cap biotechs often trade below cash value preceding Phase III announcements (past examples include Spectrum Pharmaceuticals, Ticker: SPPI; and, DepoMed, Ticker: DEPO) – this presents a huge opportunity to go long. The market is effectively valuing the opportunity at zero (or a negative value) – as such, in a strange way, this represents a "free" trade (however, don't forget you can still lose money). Finally, a high cash per share relative to price per share represents a sort of free "balance sheet hedge" and in a way diminishes the overall risk of the trade. This value (cash per share) represents a dirty liquidation value of the company. For example, lets assume Pain Therapeutics above is immediately liquidated. Shareholders would receive the net of assets and liabilities. Assume you purchased the shares at $4.90 as above – given the high cash per share your loss would not be the full $4.90 a share. Depending upon the net cash impact from the sale/payment of other assets/liabilities (and excluding legal fees, employee termination costs, etc.), your loss, as a shareholder, would likely be minimal and your liquidation proceeds would likely not deviate far from the cash per share value of $4.70.

3.2.4 Net Cash / Net Debt Balances

When analyzing the cash balances of a company, it is obviously important to factor in debt. If the company has debt, you will need to net the debt with the cash amount; that is, if the company has $100 million cash and $50 million debt, the company will have $50 million net cash ($100 cash – $50 debt). If the company has $100 million debt and $50 million cash, the company has $50 million net debt. This is a simple "liquidation method" of determining how much cash buffer the company has should they encounter a failed FDA or clinical trial related event or other financial difficulty – the point is don't simply look at cash levels. If the company has debt, focus primarily on the maturity date of the debt.[14] This information should then be compared to the expected announcement date of the catalyst event. If the catalyst falls before the maturity of the debt, and the company has net debt, and the result is negative, the implications could be catastrophic for the company and its share price. This information can obviously be factored into your trading decisions (both pre and post trade). A good example of this was with Human Genome Sciences (Ticker: HGSI). As of June 30, 2009, the company had $370 million cash and $339 million convertible notes due 2011 and 2012. In addition, the company had $247 million in lease financing (a form of "debt"). Hence, HGSI had $216 million **net debt**. The company's initial Phase III announcement date for its lupus drug was slated for July 2009. In addition, the company did not generate substantial revenues and its other drug candidates were still in development. In this situation, a failed trial would have been catastrophic for the company and a trade could have been structured to reflect this outcome (although a bearish stance would have been an abject failure).

---

[14] Debt structure (i.e. convertible, loan, bond, etc.) is important but for our purposes will be ignored as equity holder's subordination implies zero recovery in distress situations (i.e. near bankruptcy, in bankruptcy) for these types of companies.

On another trading note, a good way to assess risk for companies with publicly traded debt,[15] such as HGSI, is to follow the trading in the debt. This trading is usually confined only to credit traders on bank prop desks or hedge funds – fixed income traders are generally considered more sophisticated to equity traders on the Street (no offense to equity traders) and as such, movements in credit spreads on a company tend to foreshadow movements in the company's equity. As can be expected, HGSI's credit spreads were huge and then began to collapse (the larger the credit spread, the higher the perceived risk). Eventually it became known that HGSI was purchasing their own debt (to retire) at huge discounts – this was a good sign and foreshadowed more positive events to come. If you have access to this type of data, and you are trading a biotech with publicly traded debt, you should use it.

3.2.5 Sources of Cash

Small cap biotech companies generate cash from several sources including revenues from existing or acquired products, milestone payments or other collaborative payments, or capital raising efforts in the markets. Since most small cap biotechs generate little to no revenue, it is essential to determine how the company intends to fund itself outside of existing cash on the balance sheet.

For companies that generate revenues from existing products or acquired products, it is important to determine how stable this revenue source is and for how long. Since our trade time horizon is a year and a half or less, this information is often easy to forecast and can support your cash burn estimates. This information is usually on the Income Statement under the heading Product Revenues or Royalty Revenue and is further explained in the notes section of the financials.

---

[15] It should be noted that very few small cap biotechs have publicly traded debt (convertible bonds, high yield bonds). If you decide to trade these illiquid instruments, be very careful as you will likely be ripped off by the broker selling them to you.

Most companies have some sort of partnership agreement with a major biopharmaceutical company. These agreements include milestone payments that provide for cash payments upon successful completion of various pre-determined benchmarks during the development and testing of the drug candidate. Partnership agreements may also include various forms of R&D sharing and/or a royalty structure when/if the drug candidate is approved, amongst others elements. Companies will always make note of the key elements of their partnership agreements either on their website, in press releases or in SEC 10-Q, 10-K or 8-K filings. We will go into further detail on partnership agreements in Section 3.8: Industry Support.

The only other general source of funding available to small cap biotech companies is from the capital markets, primarily in the form of secondary equity offerings or some form of hybrid debt/quasi-equity offering that we will not cover given the variability of structures. On a trading note, secondary stock offerings, for our target universe, are generally done either immediately preceding the FDA or clinical trial related announcement (where and when the shares have gained in price substantially) or, to a lesser extent, soon after a successful announcement. Other factors which increase the probability of a secondary offering generally include low shares outstanding (i.e. under 100 million shares outstanding) and **less than a year** of cash to offset cash burn – so remember this: if your biotech company's catalyst event is near, and the share price has gained significantly, and the other factors mentioned are present, there is a high probability that the company will do a secondary offering.[16] The important elements to note regarding secondary offerings are the number of shares being issued (i.e. the impact of dilution on existing shares), the discount of the share issue and the identity of the investor(s), if known. Obviously the

---

[16] If the exact announcement date of the catalyst event is known, this may present an excellent short-term opportunity to short the stock.

smaller number of shares, the smaller the discount and the more sophisticated the investor(s) the better. As an example, I have included in Exhibit 3.4 a description of a secondary offering by Spectrum Pharmaceuticals (Ticker: SPPI).

Exhibit 3.4: Secondary Offering by Spectrum Pharmaceuticals

Original shares:	32,995,887
Share issued:	2,936,037 (excludes warrants)
Discount:	6.5% (based on price of $7.1525)
Dilution:	8.2%
Price pre-announcement:	$7.65
Price post-announcement:	$6.59
Decline (%):	13.9%
Days to trade back to pre-announcement level:	42 days

Source: SEC Form 10-Q.

On a trading note, following the secondary offering the share price will normally experience a mild to massive sell-off on the event. This is usually a good time to add to your position if you are long as the shares normally (although not always) recover to pre-secondary offering levels within a few weeks (when the catalyst announcement has still not been made). Do not read too much into these pre-catalyst sell-offs. Often traders fret that the secondary proves the impending catalyst data will be negative. This is not always the case (it also implies the company knows the outcome, is withholding it, and is thus committing fraud; an unlikely scenario despite conspiracy theories). In most cases, the company is actually doing the prudent thing by taking advantage of the elevated share price in order to raise funds which may not be available in the future should there be a failed FDA or clinical trial related outcome. Also, realize that there are informed and experienced institutional investors who purchased the shares in the secondary offering. These peoples' careers and reputation are often on the line so their investment is generally not made in haste. Relax.

3.3 OWNERSHIP

It is important to get a quick snapshot of the ownership of a small cap biotech company (or any company you intend to invest or trade in, for that matter). Shareholder data is easy to find at either the company's website or on mainstream financial websites such as Yahoo! Finance. For more detailed information and granularity, check the company's SEC Form DEF14A. The most efficient way to analyze ownership is to first look at management, then non-management/beneficial holders (greater than 5/10%) and finally institutional holders with less than 5%.

Management[17] that holds a significant equity stake in the company is usually a good sign. Generally speaking, the higher the percentage management owns, the better – a high equity ownership by management (usually and theoretically) better aligns the goals of management with the goals of the other shareholders. It is worth taking a look at SEC Form DEF14A to gain a better understanding of how management is compensated. This form provides in-depth detail on compensation, including salary, restricted stock awards, option awards, non-equity incentives and all other forms of compensation.

As an example, Exhibit 3.5 shows the Summary Compensation Table for MannKind Corp. (Ticker: MNKD) from Form DEF14A. If we look at the summary compensation table, we note that Alfred Mann is not only in management (CEO) but is also a key (if not *the* key) shareholder with a 41.7% shareholding. Following further analysis, it is discovered that he has provided significant levels of funding for the company in the past. This type of "deep

---

[17] For our purposes, management "experience" will be ignored. Although management experience is a crucial factor in the success of a company, given the large number of companies and equally large number of managers, it will be nearly impossible for an individual to accurately assess and compare management from simply reading their professional biographies. Also, past success does not necessarily guarantee future success especially within the context of the drug development process.

pocketed" shareholder is often advantageous for the funding prospects of the company – take note of these situations.

Exhibit 3.5: Summary Compensation for MannKind Corp.

Name and Principal Position	Year	Salary ($)(1)	Restricted Stock Awards ($)	Option Awards ($)(2)	Non-Equity Incentive Compensation ($)(3)	All Other Compensation ($)(4)	Total ($)
Alfred E. Mann, Chief Executive Officer and Chairman of the Board of Directors	2008	$743,077	$1,980,495	$ 212,678	$ 408,692	$ 6,594(5)	$3,351,536
	2007	$449,231	$ 707,000	$ 863,308	$ 240,339	$ 5,591	$2,265,469
	2006	$409,615	$ 746,863	$1,248,740	$ 184,327	$ 2,240	$2,591,785
Matthew J. Pfeffer (6), Corporate Vice President and Chief Financial Officer	2008	$235,577	$ 14,827	$ 48,657	$ 90,697	$ 184,468(7)	$ 574,226
Hakan S. Edstrom, President, Chief Operating Officer and Director	2008	$583,269	$1,822,018	$ 83,285	$ 296,048	$ 24,753(8)	$2,809,373
	2007	$449,231	$ 412,347	$1,002,956	$ 240,339	$ 30,639	$2,135,512
	2006	$409,615	$ 418,702	$ 905,098	$ 184,327	$ 25,508	$1,943,250
Dr. Peter Richardson, Corporate Vice President, Chief Scientific Officer	2008	$377,585	$ 728,197	$ 25,238	$ 166,137	$ 15,239(9)	$1,312,396
	2007	$359,423	$ 205,103	$ 179,070	$ 161,231	$ 13,095	$ 917,922
Juergen A. Martens, Ph.D., Corporate Vice President, Chief Technical Officer	2008	$323,577	$ 661,601	$ 25,238	$ 124,577	$ 21,849(10)	$1,156,842

Source: SEC Form DEF14A.

Another element to consider when assessing management compensation is the level of cash compensation in the form of salary and bonuses. Companies with management that take high cash salaries/bonuses relative to equity incentives should be avoided or treated with caution. Cash heavy incentives tend to give the impression (either right or wrong) that management is indirectly looting the company in the short term at the expense of longer term and equity growth oriented shareholders.

Next look at the non-management, beneficial owners. These owners will typically be (ultra-high net worth) private investors, mutual funds, hedge funds, investment banks, private equity funds, venture capital funds, pension funds and other institutional investors. It is usually worth a quick internet search on these owners (especially when they own greater than 10%) in order to understand if they are long or short term holders, what their track record is, what other biotech holdings they have (if any), if they are a specialized biotech investor or not, and if they are active or passive regarding management of the company. It is usually better (depending upon your trade perspective) to have a long term holding, (non-activist) specialist biotech fund with a solid track record as an owner than, for instance, a generalized fund with a short term focus – obviously I would want to invest side-by-side with the experts who are in for the long term than those who are simply allocating funds across a large amount of investments. Despite this, there is no guarantee that you will benefit simply because said fund is a major shareholder – there are countless examples of so-called "smart" specialist funds taking major losses on unsuccessful biotech investments. A recent example is of RA Capital Management and their significant holding in Sequenom. RA Capital is considered a sophisticated investor with a solid track record. They took a huge position in Sequenom as they considered it one of the top picks in the biotech space from the perspective of diagnostics. On one rainy day in April 2009, Sequenom issued a press release that the data on one of their key diagnostic products was "mishandled." The shares plummeted from around $15 to less than $4 in seconds where they still wallow. As you can see, even when you follow the smart money, you can lose big.

Special mention needs to be stated regarding activist hedge funds. Activist funds will target underperforming companies and take a position in order to affect "change." Although they can generate value, I suggest these types of owners be treated with extreme caution as their ultimate goal often differs from other shareholders and they may have ulterior (and unstated) motives that may be bad for your investment/trade. A high level of caution should be used when an activist hedge fund has multiple holdings in, where relevant, both the debt and equity of the company. It is not uncommon for such an activist fund to initiate an enforcement action (such as a debt maturity acceleration) on minor breaches in debt covenants thus forcing a reorganization where debt would be converted to equity (i.e. your old equity would be wiped out).

After you get an idea of the major beneficial holders, take a quick look at institutional ownership trends at www.mffais.com. This is an excellent site to quickly see trends in institutional ownership in the company's shares. The site will show you who has owned the shares, how much, if it is a new holding, if they added to or sold part of their holdings, and if they sold all of their position (amongst other data). This is often quite useful and informative as you may see top-tier funds building or exiting a position. One word of warning, however, the data comes from public records, and as such, is only a snap shot in time (that is, it does not necessarily represent the current, existing shareholding).

3.4 INSIDER ACTIVITY

Insider activity is very important as it *may* demonstrate or provide an indication of confidence or lack thereof in the company's drug candidate(s) by those closest to the company. This is (obviously) important because these people and entities have "skin in the game." During the months preceding an FDA or clinical trial related catalyst, insider activity comes under intense public scrutiny so it is something you should both focus your attention on and understand.

Insiders include executive officers, directors, or someone or something (i.e. legal entity) affiliated, as defined by the SEC, with the company. This category also includes so-called "beneficial owners" of the company, individuals or entities with greater than 10% interest in the securities of the company.[18] Insider activity is reported in numerous SEC forms including Form 3 (Initial Statement of Beneficial Ownership), Form 4 (Statement of Changes to Beneficial Ownership), Form 5 (Annual Statement of Beneficial Ownership), Form 144 (when an insider places an order to sell the company stock) and Schedule(s) 13G/13D/13GA/13DA (required filings for anyone who acquires more than 5% ownership in a company). Luckily, as you are probably aware, you do not need to compile this information for yourself at Edgar On-line (SEC filing website). Most major brokerages and mainstream financial websites, including Yahoo! Finance, compile this data for you and list it on their "insider" action/transaction areas. For Form 4s, discussed below, a very good website is SecForm4.com.

Your goal with reviewing insider transactions should be to gain a general understanding or, dare I say, "feeling," with regards to actions of the owners and management. There are no hard/concrete outputs here (aside from quantifying the net acquisitions or divestments of total insider transactions should you decide to undergo such analysis). Insider transactions are not always indicative of what the future holds. However, high insider selling is usually a stronger indication of problems ahead than the equivalent of high insider buying. There are many examples of high insider buying preceding negative FDA or clinical trial data failures so don't be fooled. High insider selling, however, sends a

---

[18] Exchange Act Rule 16a-1.

different signal, one where there is lack of confidence preceding a trial in the first place. So read into insider transactions with a high level of caution. Usually, insider transactions will not provide the bedrock from which to base your entire trade, as such, simply use this data as an analysis enhancer after your full work. The questions to ask, listed in Exhibit 3.6, are mostly common sense but they have been included for completeness.

Exhibit 3.6: Basic Questions Regarding Insider Transactions

1. What is the *general trend* of insider transactions over the past year?
    - (Significant) overall more buys than sales, i.e. 1-2x // bullish
    - (Significant) overall more sales than buys, i.e. 1-2x // bearish
    - Small to no trend // neutral

2. What is the *nature of the trend* of the divestments or acquisitions made?
    - More recent sales in increasing manner // bearish
    - More recent buys in increasing manner // bullish
    - More recent sales in decreasing manner // bullish to neutral
    - More recent buys in decreasing manner // bearish to neutral

3. How are insider transactions distributed?
    - Acquisition by several insiders during same timeframe // bullish
    - Divestment by several insiders during same timeframe // bearish
    - Sale or divestment by single insider/no clear distribution // neutral

It is often necessary to find out the nature of a *specific* insider transaction. This may be required if an insider transaction seems suspicious. For example, why did the CEO or CRO (Chief Research Officer) sell a large amount of shares prior to a major Phase III announcement? To obtain more granularity, it is usually good to check Form 4 (Statement of Changes to Beneficial Ownership) – Form 4 lists the *changes* in holdings so it is usually the best form to check for recent activity. Form 4 lists changes in insider positions that occurred in the past *2* days – hence this is near real-time regulatory data and hence of high value. This form is useful as it lists what was purchased/sold (non-derivative, such as common stock, or derivative security, such as options), when, how much, what price and the reason. Exhibits 3.7 and 3.8 provide a sample Form 4.

A Form 4 is simple to understand. It is divided into three sections: (1) Section 1 details the personal information of the individual doing the insider transaction (2) Section 2 lists non-derivative transactions, i.e. common stock and (3) Section 3 lists derivative transactions (i.e. puts, calls, warrants, options, convertible securities). The "reason" element, what I consider the most important information contained in Form 4, is listed in Table I, column "3. Transaction Code," Table II, column "4. Transaction Code," and the footnotes, which are located at the bottom of Table II under "Explanation of Responses."

Exhibit 3.7: Form 4, Sections 1 and 2

OMB APPROVAL
OMB Number: 3235-0287
Expires: February 28, 2011
Estimated average burden
hours per response....0.5

FORM 4

[ ] Check this box if no longer subject to Section 16. Form 4 or Form 5 obligations may continue. See Instruction 1(b).

UNITED STATES SECURITIES AND EXCHANGE COMMISSION
Washington, D.C. 20549

STATEMENT OF CHANGES IN BENEFICIAL OWNERSHIP OF SECURITIES

Filed pursuant to Section 16(a) of the Securities Exchange Act of 1934, Section 17(a) of the Public Utility Holding Company Act of 1935 or Section 30(f) of the Investment Company Act of 1940

1. Name and Address of Reporting Person:	2. Issuer Name and Ticker or Trading Symbol	5. Relationship of Reporting Person(s) to Issuer (Check all applicable)
Gionco David (Last) (First) (Middle) SAVIENT PHARMACEUTICALS, INC., ONE TOWER CENTER, 14TH FLOOR (Street) EAST BRUNSWICK, NJ 08816 (City) (State) (Zip)	SAVIENT PHARMACEUTICALS INC [SVNT] 3. Date of Earliest Transaction (MM/DD/YYYY) 2/27/2009 4. If Amendment, Date Original Filed (MM/DD/YYYY)	___ Director ___ 10% Owner X Officer (give title below) ___ Other (specify below) Group VP, CFO 6. Individual or Joint/Group Filing (Check Applicable Line) X Form filed by One Reporting Person ___ Form filed by More than One Reporting Person

Table I - Non-Derivative Securities Acquired, Disposed of, or Beneficially Owned

1.Title of Security (Instr. 3)	2. Trans. Date	2A. Deemed Execution Date, if any	3. Trans. Code (Instr. 8)		4. Securities Acquired (A) or Disposed of (D) (Instr. 3, 4, and 5)			5. Amount of Securities Beneficially Owned Following Reported Transaction(s) (Instr. 3 and 4)	6. Ownership Form: Direct (D) or Indirect (I) (Instr. 4)	7. Nature of Indirect Beneficial Ownership (Instr. 4)
			Code	V	Amount	(A) or (D)	Price			
Common Stock, $.01 par value per share	2/27/2009		A (1)		377	A	$3.672	46691	D	
Common Stock, $.01 par value per share	5/29/2009		A (1)		129	A	$5.3975	46720	D	
Common Stock, $.01 par value per share	8/31/2009		A (1)		62	A	$11.3475	46782	D	
Common Stock, $.01 par value per share	9/14/2009		S (2)		10887	D	$15.36 (2)	35895	D	
Common Stock, $.01 par value per share	9/15/2009		M (4)		7500	A	$4.32	43395	D	
Common Stock, $.01 par value per share	9/15/2009		S (2)		7500	D	$15.95	35895	D	

Source: SEC Form 4.

Exhibit 3.8: Form 4, Section 3 and Notes

Table II - Derivative Securities Beneficially Owned (e.g. , puts, calls, warrants, options, convertible securities)

1. Title of Derivative Security (Instr. 3)	2. Conversion or Exercise Price of Derivative Security	3. Trans. Date	3A. Deemed Execution Date, if any	4. Trans. Code (Instr. 8)		5. Number of Derivative Securities Acquired (A) or Disposed of (D) (Instr. 3, 4 and 5)		6. Date Exercisable and Expiration Date		7. Title and Amount of Securities Underlying Derivative Security (Instr. 3 and 4)		8. Price of Derivative Security (Instr. 5)	9. Number of derivative Securities Beneficially Owned Following Reported Transaction(s) (Instr. 4)	10. Ownership Form of Derivative Security: Direct (D) or Indirect (I) (Instr. 4)	11. Nature of Indirect Beneficial Ownership (Instr. 4)
				Code	V	(A)	(D)	Date Exercisable	Expiration Date	Title	Amount or Number of Shares				
Option to Purchase Common Stock, $.01 par value per share	$4.32	9/15/2009		M (3)			7500	2/6/2009	2/16/2016	Common Stock, $.01 par value per share	7500	$0	0	D	

Explanation of Responses:

(1) Consists of shares acquired pursuant to the Savient Pharmaceuticals, Inc. 1998 Employee Stock Purchase Plan, which were not previously reported on a Form 4.

(2) This sale was made pursuant to a trading plan adopted December 12, 2008 , as amended on June 26, 2009, by the reporting person in accordance with Rule 105b-1 under the Securities Exchange Act of 1934.

(3) Represents the average sale price. The highest price at which shares were sold was $15.50 and the lowest price at which shares were sold was $15.25.

(4) These options were exercised pursuant to a trading plan adopted December 12, 2008 , as amended on June 26, 2009, by the reporting person in accordance with Rule 105b-1 under the Securities Exchange Act of 1934.

Reporting Owners

Reporting Owner Name / Address	Relationships			
	Director	10% Owner	Officer	Other
Gionco David SAVIENT PHARMACEUTICALS, INC. ONE TOWER CENTER, 14TH FLOOR EAST BRUNSWICK, NJ 08816			Group VP, CFO	

Signatures

Irina Azer as Attorney-In-Fact for David Gionco	9/15/2009
** Signature of Reporting Person	Date

Reminder: Report on a separate line for each class of securities beneficially owned directly or indirectly.

* If the form is filed by more than one reporting person, *see* Instruction 4(b)(v).

** Intentional misstatements or omissions of facts constitute Federal Criminal Violations. *See* 18 U.S.C. 1001 and 15 U.S.C. 78ff(a).

Note: File three copies of this Form, one of which must be manually signed. If space is insufficient, *see* Instruction 6 for procedure.

Persons who respond to the collection of information contained in this form are not required to respond unless the form displays a currently valid OMB control number.

Source: SEC Form 4.

40

In Exhibit 3.9, I have listed the so-called Transaction Codes as defined by the SEC. These codes will tell you the general nature of the transaction. For example, a Transaction Code "P" denotes an "open market or private purchase of non-derivative or derivative security," this can be construed as bullish. A Transaction Code of "S," which denotes an open market sale, can be construed as bearish. Likewise, a Transaction Code of "M," exercise or conversion of derivative security, can be either although it is usually indicative of an insider who is exercising stock options to stock as a precursor to a sale. Codes under Rule 16b-3, in Exhibit 3.9, refer to transactions under SEC Section 16(b) that covers the "Short Swing Profit" rules applied to insiders. Section 16(b) requires, amongst other provisions contained in the Section, that company insiders return any profits made from the purchase and sale (or sale and purchase) of company securities if both transactions occur within a six month period. This is basically to prevent inside trading abuses. The SEC has adopted several exemptions to the SEC 16(b) short swing profit rule, such as 16(b)-3 ("Transactions between an Issuer and its Officers/Directors") where profit recapture provisions do not apply. Insider transactions with these codes should be taken as neutral.

Exhibit 3.9: Form 4 Transaction Codes

Code		Description	
General Transaction Codes			
P	-	Open market or private purchase of non-derivative or derivative security	Bullish
S	-	Open market or private sale of non-derivative or derivative security	Bearish
V	-	Transaction voluntarily reported earlier than required	Neutral

Source: SEC.gov/about/forms/form4data.pfd.

Exhibit 3.9: Form 4 Transaction Codes (Continued)

Code		Description	
Rule 16b-3 Transaction Codes			
A	-	Grant, award or other acquisition pursuant to Rule 16b-3(d)	Neutral
D	-	Disposition to the issuer of issuer equity securities pursuant to Rule 16b-3(e)	Neutral
F	-	Payment of exercise price or tax liability by delivering or withholding securities incident to the receipt, exercise or vesting of a security issued in accordance with Rule 16b-3	Neutral
I	-	Discretionary transaction in accordance with Rule 16b-3(f) resulting in acquisition or disposition of issuer securities	Neutral
M	-	Exercise or conversion of derivative security exempted pursuant to Rule 16b-3	Neutral
Derivatives Securities Codes (Except for transactions exempted pursuant to Rule 16b-3)			
C	-	Conversion of derivative security	See Notes
E	-	Expiration of short derivative position	Neutral
H	-	Expiration (or cancellation) of long derivative position with value received	Neutral
O	-	Exercise of out-of-the-money derivative security	See Notes
X	-	Exercise of in-the-money or at-the-money derivative security	See Notes
Other Section 16(b) Exempt Transaction and Small Acquisition Codes (except for Rule 16b-3 codes above)			
G	-	Bona fide gift	Neutral
L	-	Small acquisition under Rule 16a-6	Neutral
W	-	Acquisition of disposition by will or the laws of descent distribution	Neutral
Z	-	Deposit into or withdrawal from voting trust	Neutral
Other Transaction Codes			
J	-	Other acquisition or disposition (describe transaction)	See Notes
K	-	Transaction in equity swap or instrument with similar characteristics	See Notes
U	-	Disposition pursuant to a tender of shares in a change of control transaction	See Notes

Source: SEC.gov/about/forms/form4data.pfd.

One final note is in regards to transactions effected pursuant to Rule 10b5-1 that reference a "trading plan adopted by reporting persons." This reference will be found at the bottom of the Form 4 in the footnotes and is very important as it denotes trades that were planned well-in advance and in accordance to an adopted "trading plan" developed by the company. Hence, if you see a large insider sell/buy prior to a Phase III and in the Form 4 the sale/buy is pursuant to Rule 10b5-1 contained in the footnotes, do not concern yourself (if you are long/short) – this should be construed as neutral.[19] In Exhibit 3.8, in footnotes 2 and 4, we see that the common stock and option divestitures made by this insider (the CFO) of Savient Pharmaceuticals (Ticker: SVNT) was made pursuant to Rule 10b5-1.

Again, do not read too much into these transactions unless there is overwhelming data to prove otherwise (i.e. insider sales greatly exceed insider buys or vice versa). For example, sales by senior management may not be a negative factor if these individuals hold a sizeable position in the shares of the company. It is possible, and not particularly unreasonable, that the insider is diversifying their personal assets even if not under a trading plan (i.e. the transaction is an outright sale). Again, if your suspicion is drawn, check the Form 4 to gain a better understanding of the reason behind the transaction – this is a preferable route than listening to market rumors about insider activity.

Finally, it is important to mention that large sales/buys (i.e. around 1 ~ 5% of total shares outstanding) by major beneficial holders, especially specialty hedge funds or other institutional holders (banks, mutual funds) need to be carefully scrutinized. Although not always the situation, a large sale by one of these types of insiders could be a sign of serious trouble ahead. On the other hand, the

---

[19] It should be noted that the language in Rule 10b5-1 contains a loophole where a planned trade can be cancelled and as such, since there was no trade, insider trading provisions do not apply.

opposite may be true for large buys. If you encounter this situation, do a news search of the fund and the name of the biotech company and see what information you get, if any. See if the investor is also selling/buying stakes in other similar companies – this information can be found by searching under the entity's legal name (or fund's legal name) under mffais.com. If you are concerned, do an additional amount of due diligence.

3.5   ANALYST VIEW

It is valuable to assess how analysts view a particular biotech company especially prior to an FDA or clinical trial event. The most useful information to cull from analysts during a FRS process is (1) the stock price target for both successful *and* unsuccessful catalyst outcomes and (2) the timing of said announcement, where relevant (i.e. assuming an exact date has not been set).

Regarding price target estimates, analysts will generally be accurate given the significant amount of time and research they spend when assessing market potential of the drug candidate, their discussions with executive management in addition to conversations with industry insiders and specialists. It goes without saying that you will probably not be able to assess a price target range better than most analysts.

Analysts will often (although not always) provide a more precise estimate of when FDA or clinical trial data will be announced. This can be attributed to the analyst's knowledge of FDA timelines or trial procedures and time elements within a trial's structure. Companies usually provide a very rough estimate of when they expect results to be announced (for example, "fourth quarter," "mid-year," "late in third quarter," "early October"). More specific information on the date of the announcement is absolutely vital as it will allow you to structure the optimal position well in advance.

Both the price target range and timing information can and should be used to help guide the trade structure you will eventually use. For example, analysts covering ABC stock, which currently trades at $7.50, estimate a successful trial will result in a price of $12.00 per share and an unsuccessful trial will result in a price of $1.00 per share. Analysts expect the announcement to be in *mid*-November. Using this information, you would structure your option strategies using the $1.00/$12.00 range as an initial guidepost for bullish, bearish or neutral strategies (depending upon the results of your own analysis). Also, you would need to make a decision whether or not to structure your strategy in the November or December options. This can be very important as you may structure a net long position in November options and the ultimate result could occur in the fourth week of November (hence, your November options will have already expired). Although you may have made money on the increase in volatility (Vega) and price (Delta) preceding the announcement, you will not be involved in the "action" during the actual announcement, and thus you will miss either the substantial gain or fall of the shares (which could be either positive or negative depending on what strategy you employed). Of course, you could have played it this way on the short volatility side, where you would have been net short with the expectation that the announcements would be *after* expiration, thus generating you extremely high returns by selling, the now worthless, high volatility November options – a high risk strategy indeed, but very profitable. As you can see, the trade permutations are virtually unlimited.

You may now think that I completely trust analysts – to put it simply, I don't (nor should you). As stated, I only trust them with regards to **price range estimates** and **timing** of announcement estimates. Regarding trial success estimates (i.e. the trial will be a success or failure or outcome of FDA-related decisions), however, I tend to discount what analysts say simply because they are usually wrong. This is not to say that their analysis is flawed – elements of it are usually quite good as already discussed. It is simply a statement that it is literally impossible for analysts to accurately predict which trials will be successful and which will be failures given the significant complexity and number of variables involved – it is often nearly a coin toss. Given that most trials fail, most analysts err on the conservative side by "predicting" a failure. The same can be said for FDA decisions or outcomes of Advisory Panels.

Case in point, among the largest biotech success stories in the past several years, Dendreon and Human Genome Sciences, the analyst consensus for both was total failure. If you listened to the analysts, you would have been on the sidelines and missed out on over 500% gains. Likewise, two high profile FDA Panels for diet drugs in 2010 resulted in near opposite outcomes to analyst consensus – Vivus' Qnexa was expected to pass (it failed) and Orexigen's Contrave was expected to fail (it passed!). There are countless other examples where consensus proved to be wrong. Be cognizant of this feature of small cap biotech catalyst trading and prepare with a sense of skepticism with regards to consensus thought.

3.6 TECHNICAL ANALYSIS

It is important to take a look at a company's charts when approaching a catalyst event. If you are a big proponent of technical analysis (I am), you need to realize that the technical analysis "rules" as applied to non-biotech companies do not apply to biotech companies *with an approaching catalyst event*. Nearing such an event, most, if not all, technical indicators become meaningless – at this point, the only thing that matters is the binary announcement. As such, do not read too much into daily price action – it will be volatile.

When using technical analysis, the only useful information is with regards to *prior trading levels within the past several years (ideally 5 years) on the same/similar catalyst*. For example, it is quite common for a company to have had a Phase III failure where the FDA required additional data (which is achieved through several additional years of studies). When this happens, the company's stock will have sold-off substantially. A 3 to 5-year chart will often quickly identify said past events. The important data to cull from this information is the price level prior to the announcement and the level immediately after. This data, in most cases, can give you an idea where the price *should*[20] trade prior to the most immediate trial announcement in addition, where applicable, to the level where it will likely trade after another failure (this downside value will often be a minimum value, as a second failed Phase III study, depending on the individual circumstance of the company, will often prove fatal to the company).

A perfect recent example of using prior trading levels is Dendreon (Ticker: DNDN). Several years ago, in May 2007, the FDA stated that one of the company's leading Phase III drug candidates targeting prostate cancer, required additional tests prior to approval. Prior to this news, the stock traded from around $4.50 a share to as high as $25.00 a share on excitement regarding the drug's blockbuster potential. The FDA's negative decision sent the shares plummeting back to around $5.00 a share. In April 2009, Dendreon having worked several years on addressing the FDA's issues, once again prepared to announce Phase III results. Prior to the announcement, the shares traded up from $5.00 to $7.00 a share. Phase III announcement was positive sending the shares back to the twenties.[21] In this case, historic technical levels proved quite accurate and useful.

If you use prior technical levels in your analysis, it is important to be cognizant of the need to adjust for the impact of share dilution on the company's market

---

[20] Assuming the market value of the drug candidate has not experienced dramatic change.
[21] Dendreon issued net 18 million shares in the interim period; the market value of the company for both periods was approximately the same.

capitalization. For example, stock XYZ's shares traded at $5.00 with 10 million shares outstanding (for a market capitalization of $50 million) immediately preceding an FDA decision on the company's late stage drug candidate.[22] The result was negative (i.e. a "Complete Response Letter") and XYZ's shares crashed to $1.00. Several years later the company announced that it would release new top-line data on the same drug candidate in about six months. Since the failure, however, the company issued 10 million shares of common stock. The shares now trade at $2.00 (for a market capitalization of $40 million; i.e. 20 million shares x $2.00 a share). Assuming the value of the drug candidate has not changed materially, it would be misguided to assume that the shares should trade to $5.00, the prior technical level. Why? Because that would place the value of the drug candidate at nearly double its former value, i.e. $100 million versus $50 million. A more appropriate analysis would be to assume the former value, $50 million, and divide by fully diluted shares outstanding, 20 million, which would yield an initial run-up price of around $2.50. The point is: don't ignore the impact of share dilution if you use prior technical levels in your analysis.

One final word with respect to the use of technical analysis: be cognizant of other corporate actions, such as stock splits (especially reverse stock splits) on price history. For example, if one looks at the price history of Adventrx (Ticker: ANX) during 2010, it seems as though ANX was at a time a $12.00 stock. This is not true – Adventrx did a 25-for-1 reverse stock split which converted the sub-$0.50 penny stock to one that now trades near $2.00. Don't assume the stock is going "back" to $12.00. If you see huge price spikes and massive volatility on a

---

[22] In this example, I assume XYZ has only one drug candidate.

1-year chart, the stock in question probably did a reverse stock split and should be viewed with an additional level of scrutiny.[23]

3.7 PIPELINE

A company's pipeline includes all existing drug development programs the company is working on. This may include pre-clinical trials, Phase I and Phase II trials and finally Phase III and all categories of post Phase III products/candidates. A company's pipeline can be found on their website, usually with an explicit link to the data which is often displayed as a chart. It is often useful to print out the pipeline page, make any appropriate notes and file in your database for future reference. Companies that avoid listing their pipeline typically only have drug candidates in pre-clinical and Phase I trials – avoid these companies.

When analyzing a company's pipeline, first focus on their Phase III candidates. For each candidate listed, there is usually a link to information regarding more detailed data about the drug, trial structure, the status of the Phase III trial and sometimes (although not always) the estimated completion and reporting of data from the Phase III trial. The key information at this juncture is to determine when the results of the trial are expected. If this is not stated on the website check the company's most recent quarterly (or annual) earnings statement. If the timing is still not estimated, it is likely that the results are slated for a point in time more than 1 to 2 years – you should make a note of this and file this company under potential future opportunities. It is likely that there will not be options available to trade on the name during the time frame (and if there are, the spreads will kill any successful trade) and as such you will need to buy the stock. Again, the event catalyst is too far in the future, so I suggest you move to

---

[23] Companies that do reverse stock splits, mainly to satisfy exchange minimum price listing requirements, are often (although not always) in some sort of distress and should be avoided.

another company. Next, take a quick look at the other Phase II and Phase I programs and make a note of timing if available. As an example, Exhibit 3.10 displays the pipeline of XYZ Corporation, a company focused on the development of drugs in the oncology (i.e. cancer) space. This chart and its associated links provides an excellent snap-shot to get an idea about what drugs XYZ is developing and what stages each specific drug is in.

Exhibit 3.10: XYZ Corporation Pipeline

PRODUCT	PRECLINICAL	PHASE 1	PHASE 2	PHASE 3
XYZ-100 _Lung cancer_	▨▨▨▨▨▨▨▨▨▨▨▨▨▨▨▨▨▨			
XYZ-150 _Colon cancer_	▨▨▨▨▨▨▨▨▨▨▨▨▨▨▨			
XYZ-200 _Bladder cancer_	▨▨▨▨▨▨▨▨▨▨▨▨▨▨▨			
XYZ-250 _Leukemia_	▨▨▨▨▨▨▨▨▨			
Other programs	▨▨▨▨			

From the chart above, we can quickly identify that this company has one Phase III candidate (XYZ-100 which targets lung cancer). Our next move should be to identify when the key date for information is expected. Clicking on XYZ-100, we identify the trial history of the drug candidate but there is no information on result dates. Next we check news under Investor Relations part of their website. The best place is a recent quarterly earnings announcement. In the 2Q'09 earnings press release, under Corporate Progress and Guidance, we find the following statement:

"We expect to report top-line results from the XYZ-100 Phase III trials on November 5, 2009. If the top-line results are positive, we plan to submit a New Drug Application with the FDA by year-end, targeting approval and commercial launch of XYZ-100 in 2010."

We now have an exact action date (hopefully) – our work on this aspect of our analysis is now complete. Make a note of the other drug candidates and move to the next part of our analysis.

Exhibit 3.11: ABC Pharmaceuticals Pipeline

PRODUCT	PRECLINICAL	PHASE 1	PHASE 2	PHASE 3
ABC-1X *Thyroid cancer*	██████████████████████████████████████			
ABC-2X *Non-Hodgkin Lymphoma*	████████████████████			
ABC-3X *Melanoma*	███████████████████			
ABC-4X *Leukemia*	██████████			
Other programs	████████			

A potential red flag, depending on your point of view, is a company with a few early stage product candidates and/or a single Phase III product candidate – a failed trial in these situations (or an adverse FDA related decision) will often result in significant share declines. This type of situation should factor prominently into the trade structure you use. ABC Pharmaceuticals provides an example of this situation. Looking at the company's pipeline in Exhibit 3.11, we see that they have a single Phase III drug candidate and several Phase I candidates. Upon searching, we see that Phase III pivotal data is due for mid-June 2010. Looking at their financials, we note that cash at the current burn rate will only sustain the company into 3Q'10 (as of 1Q'10) – hence, this is a make or break situation for the company. A failed Phase III could result in several additional years of trials requiring significant financial resources (which the company does not have). As the company only has one Phase III and a few Phase I candidates, important strategic decisions will need to be made if there is a failed Phase III. For example, the company will need to assess if they can adequately address issues related to the failure. Also, the company may need to terminate Phase I trials on other candidates in order to conserve funds. This is a very ugly situation – make sure you understand a company's pipeline and implications for failed late stage trials or adverse FDA decisions.

3.8 INDUSTRY SUPPORT

It is important to assess what industry partnerships, if any, the company maintains for the development of select drugs in its pipeline. The backing of a major biopharmaceutical company such as Glaxo, Novartis, Merck, Abbot or Pfizer, for example, provides not only legitimacy/credibility to the company's product potential, but also experience with ushering the drug through the various phases of drug development (hence theoretically improving the probability of success) and financial (through milestone payments and other collaborative revenues), commercial and/or marketing incentives leading up to and after drug approval. Post approval, the partnership may result in the partner acquiring the company.

The best place to find information on the company's partnership(s) is usually under its pipeline information area on its website. This will generally be a starting point to gain information regarding the nature of the partnership. For more detailed information check the quarterly press releases or in the 10-Q and the 10-K.

Partnerships, collaborative agreements and other types of structures (collectively, "partnerships") will generally contain up to four parts: up-front cash payments, various milestone payments for achievement of specific clinical and/or regulatory goals, R&D expense sharing, and post-approval royalty agreements. The key element to focus on in the partnership agreement, for our purposes, is the amount and timing of the milestone payments. As the company progresses in the drug development process, the milestone payments contained in the partnership agreement obviously become more and more important due to continued cash burn experienced by the company. As mentioned in Section 3.2.2: Cash Burn, it is important to get a handle on where the company is with regards to expected timing of achieving a milestone payment and the amount of cash available to bridge this time gap. Again, this information will almost always be listed (either directly or indirectly) in quarterly earnings announcements or in the 10-Q or 10-K.

An example industry partnership is Pain Therapeutics' (Ticker: PTIE) agreement with King Pharmaceuticals (Ticker: KG) for the development of one of their drug candidates. The company entered into a strategic alliance with King back in 2005. The structure of the strategic alliance is contained both under the pipeline portion of their website and in SEC filings (10-K, 10-Q, 8-K) and provides good information to assess potential value of their drug candidate with success. For example, terms of the agreement include a $150 million up-front cash payment, $150 million in clinical and regulatory milestones and $100 million in research and development expenses. In addition, the agreement calls for a 20% royalty on product sales amongst other elements.

When evaluating a *just* announced partnership deal, do not be deceived by the initial (often big) headline number – most of the value may be back-ended (via clinical and regulatory milestone and/or royalty agreements) and is thus uncertain, whether or not the company will ever capture it. The biggest immediate impact on the share price will be from an up-front cash payment as this immediately and directly contributes value. For example, if XYZ stock announces a $250 million partnership deal, of which $50 million is an up-front cash payment, and the company has 25 million shares, XYZ stock should trade up between $1 to $2 per share ($50mln / 25mln = $2). Milestone payments, R&D expense sharing, and royalty amounts, although important, will normally have lesser *immediate* impact (this obviously may or may not hold true depending upon the situation).

A partnership with a major biopharmaceutical is a potential success enhancer and can add immediate and sustained value to the small cap biotech company in the form of cash payments and other types of support. By no means, however, should one assume that it guarantees success – again, within the scope of small cap biotech trading, the outcome is never a certainty.

3.9 CONCLUSION

If you spent at least a few minutes on each topic in the FRS, you have taken the important first step in developing a successful trade.   At this juncture you should have some idea regarding the strengths and weaknesses of each company in the trade universe. Using this knowledge should improve the probability of a successful trade as it will provide you with an idea whether or not you should approach the trade with a bearish, bullish or neutral stance in addition to having some idea at what price level(s) and at what time period(s) to structure your trade.

CHAPTER 4.0

OPTION BASICS

4.1 OVERVIEW

This chapter is structured to provide an overview of options from a *trading* perspective. The primary goal is to provide the reader a conceptual understanding of how options work and how they can be used to make money. For this reason, this chapter will not include arcane theoretical discussions on option pricing, mathematical models, etc. – I'll leave that to the academics. I intend to focus on what you need to know to trade options in real life situations. If you already have a solid grasp of options, feel free to skip this section and move to Chapter 5: Trading Strategy & Tactics.

4.2 CONCEPTUAL FRAMEWORK

It may surprise you, but an option is very easy to understand. In its most basic form, an option is an exchange-traded contract between two individuals to either buy or sell the stock of a company (the "Underlying" Stock) at a specific price (the "Strike" Price) until the contract expires (the "Expiration" Date). For this right, the buyer of the option *pays* and the seller of the option *receives*, an amount of cash known as the "Premium."

There are two types of options: the "Put" and the "Call." A Put is the option (held by the buyer) to *sell* the Underlying stock at a specific Strike Price until the Expiration Date.[24] A Call is the option (held by the buyer) to *buy* the Underlying stock at a specific Strike Price until the Expiration Date. An option is thus defined and identified by these four elements: Underlying Stock, Expiration Date, Strike Price and Type (Put or Call).

Exhibit 4.1: Key Option Terms

Underlying	The stock on which the option trades
Strike	The price at which an option buyer can purchase (Call) or sell (Put) the Underlying stock
Expiration	The date the option expires
Premium	The amount the option buyer pays or the option seller receives for the option
Put	The option to sell the Underlying at the Strike by Expiration
Call	The option to buy the Underlying at the Strike by Expiration

For every Put Buyer there is a Put Seller. Likewise, for every Call Buyer there is a Call Seller. You, as an individual trader/investor, can choose to be a Put Buyer, a Put Seller, a Call Buyer or a Call Seller – these are the four fundamental option positions.[25]

At the most basic level, a trader (or investor) chooses to buy or sell Puts or Calls to gain a specific risk exposure in an Underlying stock in order to capture a desired return. This is similar to the motives of a stock trader and/or investor. For example, if an investor likes ABC stock, the investor will buy ABC stock (i.e. gain a long or bullish risk exposure to ABC stock) with the desire that ABC stock increases in price (thus capturing a desired return). Likewise, if a trader is negative on ABC stock, the trader will sell short the stock (i.e. gain a short or bearish risk exposure to ABC stock) with the desire that ABC stock decreases in

---

[24] Note that in each case, the right granted by the option is just that, an option (and not an obligation) to buy or sell the stock at the Strike Price until Expiration.

[25] Of course these positions can be combined to form more complex positions – but these are the fundamental component parts.

price. Using stock, the choice for an *opening* position is limited to either buy or to sell short. Options, however, greatly expand risk exposure choices. Below I list these choices and the sentiment they represent for the four fundamental positions:[26]

- A Put Buyer is Bearish on the Underlying stock[27]
- A Put Seller is Neutral to Bullish
- A Call Buyer is Bullish
- A Call Seller is Neutral to Bearish

4.2.1 Option Buyer versus Option Seller

It is very important to understand the concept of *Option Buying* versus *Option Selling* and the implications with regards to initial P&L,[28] risk and return. Here is the difference:

An Option Buyer:

- *Pays* money to initiate the trade (i.e. the individual Buys the option, either a Put or a Call, at the Ask)
- Risk is *defined* and equal to the amount paid to initiate the trade
- Return is *undefined*

An Option Seller:

- *Receives* money to initiate the trade (i.e. the individual Sells the option, either a Put or a Call, at the Bid)
- Risk is *undefined*
- Return is *defined* and equal to the amount received to initiate the trade

---

[26] Our initial focus will be on the *direction* of the Underlying stock (i.e. up or down). It should be noted, however, that there are many other ways to make money with options, such as an increase or decrease in volatility. These approaches will be covered later on in the book.

[27] Bearish means the individual expects the Underlying stock to decline in price; Bullish means the individual expects the Underlying stock to increase in price; Neutral means the individual expects the Underlying price to neither increase nor decrease.

[28] Initial P&L is the cash flow movement, either positive or negative, to initiate the trade. For example, if I buy an option, I would pay money and therefore this represents a cash outflow. If I sell an option, I would receive money and therefore this represents a cash inflow.

The distinction is clear and unambiguous: an Option Buyer pays cash up-front for the potential to generate undefined returns (in certain situations, theoretically unlimited returns) while risking the amount paid while an Option Seller receives cash up-front for the potential to keep this cash while taking an undefined risk (in certain situations, theoretically unlimited risk).

4.2.2 The Option Chain

A good way to learn about options is to study the topic in the actual format used in a real-life trading situation: from the Option Chain. **When you trade options, you will trade from Option Chains contained on your broker's website.** Exhibit 4.2 provides an example of a basic Option Chain for ABC stock for the August "Series" as displayed by a major broker. A Series includes all of the options (i.e. all Strikes for both Puts and Calls) with the same Expiration month. For example, the August Series includes all options that expire in the month of August.

Exhibit 4.2: Option Chain for ABC Stock

Stock: ABC @ $82.92
Today: June 2, 2010
SERIES: AUGUST

CALLS					PUTS			
BID	ASK	Volume	O.I.	STRIKE	BID	ASK	Volume	O.I.
14.25	14.50	4	152	AUG 70.0	1.75	1.82	280	6,947
10.30	10.50	19	454	AUG 75.0	2.75	2.83	40	250
6.85	7.00	248	2,015	AUG 80.0	4.30	4.40	133	4,404
4.15	4.25	1,353	3,332	AUG 85.0	6.55	6.65	1,071	2,597
2.24	2.31	570	8,992	AUG 90.0	9.55	9.90	0	762

At the most basic level, an Option Chain lists the Bid and the Ask prices for both the Puts and Calls for each Strike in a Series. A basic Option Chain will also include Volume and Open Interest ("OI"). Most brokerages allow you to customize Option Chains (by including, for example, the Greeks or levels of implied volatility, both to be discussed later in this Chapter) but the most basic elements are those listed in Exhibit 4.2.

The Bid and Ask are the *current market prices* for either the Calls or the Puts (this is the "Premium" value mentioned previously). The Bid is the current market price to Sell the option, and the Ask is the current market price to Buy the option. It should be noted that this differs from the "Last" price, which was the last price where the option traded – this could have been seconds ago, or possibly months ago. Never trade using the "Last" quote, always use the Bid or Ask – this is obvious but still merits mention and emphasis. Let's do a few basic trades using the data contained in the Option Chain in Exhibit 4.3:

Exhibit 4.3: Option Chain for XYZ Stock

Stock: XYZ @ $16.35
Today: June 2, 2010
SERIES: SEPTEMBER

CALLS					PUTS			
BID	ASK	Volume	O.I.	STRIKE	BID	ASK	Volume	O.I.
2.83	2.88	10	2,114	SEP 14.0	0.59	0.61	455	3,144
2.08	**2.13**	242	1,071	SEP 15.0	0.83	0.86	247	7,365
1.44	1.48	564	1,389	SEP 16.0	1.19	1.22	306	6,256
0.92	0.96	576	2,267	SEP 17.0	1.68	1.71	1,103	3,633
0.55	0.57	2,192	4,435	SEP 18.0	2.30	2.34	482	1,594

If I want to buy 10 XYZ SEP 15.0 Strike Calls, I would check XYZ stock's September Option Chain. At this moment, the SEP 15.0 Strike Call (bolded) is trading at 2.08 Bid / 2.13 Ask (like a stock price, Premium values, i.e. the Bid or Ask, are constantly changing). Since I wish to buy the Call, I would pay 2.13 per contract (the "ASK"). Here is the (very simple) math:

= Premium x # of Contracts x Multiplier[29] = Total Cost (not including commissions)

... in numbers:

= 2.13 x 10 x 100 = $2,130

Hence, I would pay $2,130 (Debit) to initiate this trade. Let's say, for example, that I wish to *sell* 10 XYZ SEP 15.0 Strike Calls. In this situation, I would sell the option at 2.08 per contract (the "BID"). Here is the math for this situation:

= 2.08 x (10) x 100 = ($2,080)

"( )" denotes selling and hence a Credit. In this example I would receive $2,080 for selling these Calls. If I want to buy 30 XYZ SEP 14.0 Strike Puts, I would check the XYZ Option Chain again. At this moment, the SEP 14.0 Strike Put is trading at 0.59 Bid / 0.61 Ask. Since I wish to buy the Put, I would pay 0.61 per contract. Here is the math:

= Premium x # of Contracts x Multiplier = Total Cost

= 0.61 x 30 x 100 = $1,830

Hence, I would pay $1,830 (Debit). For a final example, let's say that I wish to *sell* 30 XYZ SEP 14.0 Strike Puts. In this situation, I would sell the option at 0.59 per contract. Here is the math for this situation:

= 0.59 x (30) x 100 = ($1,770)

In this example, I would receive $1,770 for selling these Puts. Easy, right?

---

[29] A multiplier denotes how many Underlying is represented by 1 option contract. For equity options (i.e. options on common stock), the multiplier is usually 100 which means 1 option contract represents 100 Underlying shares. At times the option multiplier will be different – this is primarily due to corporate actions such as a stock split. Your broker should note this on their Option Chains if applicable.

4.2.3 The Importance of Understanding The Bid / Ask Spread

In both situations above, since we purchased/sold at the market Bid/Ask quote, our P&L immediately following the trade would show a loss. If you have never traded options, and the Bid/Ask spread is wide, and you trade at the Bid/Ask, you may be shocked (at the immediate negative P&L impact in your brokerage account). This is due to the fact that there is a "spread" that you need to "pay." This is the Bid/Ask spread, which basically (supposedly) compensates the market maker for taking the risk (or taking the "other side") of doing your trade.

For the 10 XYZ SEP 15.0 Strike Call example in Exhibit 4.3, the Bid/Ask spread is 0.05 wide (= 2.13 – 2.08 = 0.05). In actual dollars and cents for the trade, this equates to $50 (= 0.05 x 10 x 100 = $50). Depending upon how your brokerage quotes your position, you will show an immediate loss on your trade of either $50 (if your broker quotes the price to exit the trade, i.e. if you are long, the price to get out and if you are short, the price to cover) or $25 (if your broker quotes on a mid-price basis, i.e. the average of the current Bid/Ask). For 10 ABC AUG 90.0 Strike Put (Exhibit 4.2), the Bid/Ask spread is 0.35 wide (= 9.90 – 9.55 = 0.35) which equates to an immediate negative P&L hit of $175 (= 0.35/2 x 10 x 100) for a mid-price basis quote.[30]

---

[30] It should be noted that if your broker quotes on a mid-point basis you may experience "Phantom P&L," i.e. P&L from failed positions may still be counted as having value. For example, a failed 100 Call position will still be worth $250 if it is quoted as 0.00 Bid / 0.05 Ask (= (0.00+0.05)/2 x 100 x 100) – when the Calls expire worthless, you will lose this money following expiration and the loss will be reflected in your brokerage account.

Exhibit 4.4: Initial P&L Impact of Bid/Ask Spread

Trade: Buy 10 XYZ SEP 15.0 Strike Call

Spread	Position	Total Spread Value
Bid 2.08 / Ask 2.13 = 0.05 (= 2.13 - 2.08)	10	$50 (= 0.05 x 10 x 100)

P&L Impact:

Mid-point basis:	$25 (= 0.05/2 x 10 x 100)
Cost-to-exit basis:	$50 (= 0.05 x 10 x 100)

Trade: Sell 10 ABC AUG 90.0 Strike Put

Spread	Position	Total Spread Value
Bid 9.55 / Ask 9.90 = 0.35 (= 9.90 – 9.55)	10	$350 (= 0.35 x 10 x 100)

P&L Impact:

Mid-point basis:	$175 (= 0.35/2 x 10 x 100)
Cost-to-exit basis:	$350 (= 0.05 x 10 x 100)

The spreads for XYZ and ABC, however, are not that wide. In certain illiquid situations (nearly all situations in small cap biotech), however, the spread can be extremely wide to seemingly pointless/outrageous. For example, Omeros Corp. (Ticker: OMER) AUG 2010 5.0 Strike Put as of this date is trading at 0.00 Bid / 4.90 Ask (a spread of 4.90) with the stock trading at $5.46. This is a completely ridiculous quote – only a fool would trade at this level. If I were to buy this Put, it means that I would be willing to pay $4.90 to get $0.10 of downside protection – also, I would take an *immediate* $2,450 loss if I purchased 10 contracts! If I were to sell this Put (as an opening trade), it means that I would be selling the option for zero thus taking a full $5.00 of downside risk – I would get paid absolutely nothing to take all the risk, a true sucker's bet if there ever was one. This quote is actually an "open invitation" to make a "fair" offer on the option (either on the Bid or Ask side).

The examples just discussed demonstrate the absolute importance of assessing the Bid/Ask spread *prior to initiating a trade* – don't get blind-sided by the spread. In Section 5.6: Never Trade at the Bid or Ask, I discuss strategies how to minimize the amount of spread you need to pay – this knowledge alone will save you thousands of dollars.

4.2.4 Volume and Open Interest

As mentioned, the other basic information included in an Option Chain is Volume and Open Interest. Volume is easy to understand: it represents the total number of options traded for each Strike during a day (just as the volume for a stock represents the total number of shares traded during a day). For example, the SEP 16.0 Strike Call volume as of this day, June 2, was 564 contracts (see Exhibit 4.3). This means that 564 contracts (options) were bought/sold during the day. On the same day the SEP 18.0 Strike Call traded 2,192 contracts, the most active strike for this Series. Volume is a very useful metric as it shows where most of the trading action for the day is occurring. Many inferences can be made reading daily volume data. This will be discussed in further detail in Section 5.11: Monitor Option Activity Pre-Catalyst.

While volume represents the *daily* activity for each option, Open Interest represents the net increase or decrease in the total number of options traded (opened and closed) *since the inception of the Series*. For example, the Open Interest for the XYZ SEP 18.0 Strike Calls in Exhibit 4.3 is 4,435. This means that a net total of 4,435 option contracts have been opened/remain open since the Series inception. It is important to note that daily Volume does not always equate to Open Interest – that is, just because a day's Volume was, for example, 500 contracts, it does not mean that Open Interest will increase by 500 contracts. To expand this point, Exhibit 4.5 shows daily Volume, Open Interest and Net Change for the ABC 5.0 Strike Calls. On Day 1, Open Interest was 10,000 contracts – a net total of 10,000 ABC 5.0 Strike Calls have been opened (and remain open). During Day 1, 500 contracts traded. On Day 2, Open Interest is now 10,500 contracts, which means all of the Volume on Day 1 was from new (initial) contracts.[31]   On Day 2, contract Volume is 300.   On Day 3, Open

Interest is now 10,700, a net increase of 200 contracts.   This means that of the

300 contract Volume during Day 2, 100 were closing positions and 200 were

opening (initial) positions.   During Day 3, 1,500 contracts trade.   On Day 4,

Open Interest declines by 1,500 contracts, the entire Volume experienced on

Day 3.

Exhibit 4.5: Open Interest and Volume

ABC 5.0 Strike Calls	Volume	Open Interest	Net Change
Day 1 (open)	- 0 -	10,000	
Day 1 (close)	500		
Day 2 (open)	- 0 -	10,500	(a) +500
Day 2 (close)	300		
Day 3 (open)	- 0 -	10,700	(b) +200
Day 3 (close)	1,500		
Day 4 (open)	- 0 -	9,200	(c) -1,500

Open Interest is a very useful metric as it gives you a snapshot into the money

flow in the various Strikes of both Puts and Calls.   This can at times allow you

to gauge general sentiment in the Underlying shares.   In some situations, it is

extremely important to actively monitor **and** interpret Open Interest – this is

covered in Section 5.11.

4.2.5 Option Expiration

Before we continue, it is important to quickly discuss the finer points of Option

Expiration.   Options expire on the Saturday immediately following the 3rd

Friday of the expiration month.[32]   This sounds confusing but it is not – if you

look at a calendar, it is quite simple.   The September 2010 Series expire on

---

[31] Open Interest data is available the following day. Hence Volume that occurs today
will be reflected in Open Interest tomorrow. A net increase/decrease from this data can
thus be calculated.

[32] Options stop trading on the 3rd Friday; they, however, expire on the following day:
Saturday.

Saturday September 18, 2010 – which happens to be the Saturday following the 3rd Friday in the month of September. This construct is true for all months in the year. Make sure you don't think in terms of the expiration being in the 3rd *week* of the month. For example, Exhibit 4.6 compares the September 2010 and January 2011 Series in terms of Expiration week. Options for the September 2010 Expiration expire in the 3rd week. Options for the January 2011 Series, however, expire on Saturday the 22nd. Technically, this falls on the *fourth* week in the month of January. Don't make this mistake: if you stick to the 3rd Friday concept, you can't go wrong. Your broker website should list the expiration date for each Series should there be any confusion.

Exhibit 4.6: September 2010 and January 2011 Series

SEPTEMBER 2010								JANUARY 2011						
Week	M	T	W	T	F	S	S		M	T	W	T	F	S	S
1			1	2	3	4	5							1	2
2	6	7	8	9	10	11	12		3	4	5	6	7	8	9
3rd	13	14	15	16	17	18	19		10	11	12	13	14	15	16
4th	20	21	22	23	24	25	26		17	18	19	20	21	22	23
5	27	28	29	30					24	25	26	27	28	29	30
6									31						

☐ = Options Stop Trading
■ = Options Expire

Attention to such a seemingly small detail may appear unimportant but nothing can be further from the truth – knowing **exactly** when a Series expires is extremely important when planning trades in the small cap biotech space – it can either cost or save you thousands of dollars. You absolutely must know this information.

4.2.6 Intrinsic and Extrinsic Value

An option's value is divided into two segments: intrinsic value and time value (also referred to as extrinsic value). Intrinsic value is the amount the Strike Price is below the Stock Price (for Calls) and the amount the Strike Price is above the Stock Price (for Puts). In certain situations, intrinsic value is equal to zero. Extrinsic Value is the extra amount of the option's value that is not Intrinsic Value. In certain situations the Extrinsic Value comprises the total value of the option. For example, Exhibit 4.7 lists the Option Chain for the November Series for EFG stock. The NOV 45.0 Strike Call is currently trading at 4.55 Bid / 4.60 Ask with EFG at $47.26. The intrinsic value of this Call is 2.26 (= $47.26 – 45.0). The extrinsic value of this Call (using the Ask price) is 2.34 (= 4.60 – 2.26). Now let's look at the 49.0 Strike Call. In this situation, the intrinsic value is zero – the 49.0 Strike is greater than EFG's stock price. As such, the entire option is comprised of extrinsic value, which equals 2.38 (again, using the Ask price).

Exhibit 4.7: Option Chain for EFG Stock

Stock: EFG @ $47.26
Today: July 14, 2010
SERIES: NOVEMBER

CALLS					PUTS			
BID	ASK	Volume	O.I.	STRIKE	BID	ASK	Volume	O.I.
4.55	4.60	20	1,365	NOV 45.0	2.36	2.40	40	1,239
3.90	4.00	67	1,286	NOV 46.0	2.73	2.77	76	2,457
3.30	3.40	35	785	NOV 47.0	3.15	3.20	399	1,133
2.81	2.86	800	2,679	NOV 48.0	3.60	3.65	560	3,911
2.34	2.38	385	1,736	NOV 49.0	4.10	4.20	80	1,355

Let's look at the Puts. The NOV 48.0 Strike Put is currently trading at 3.60 Bid / 3.65 Ask again with EFG at $47.26. The intrinsic value of this Put is 0.74 (= 48.0 - $47.26). The extrinsic value (using the Ask price) is 2.91 (= 3.65 – 0.74). Now let's look at the 46.0 Strike Put. In this situation, the intrinsic value is zero – the 46.0 Strike is less than EFG's stock price. As such, the entire option is comprised of extrinsic value, which equals 2.77 (again, using the Ask price).

The knowledge of an option's intrinsic and extrinsic value is usually most important prior to executing a trade. This is a quick and simple way to double-check your trade to avoid any (obvious) errors or poor trading decisions. For example, the FEB'11 6.0 Strike Call of Sangamo BioSciences (Ticker: SGMO) was trading at 1.15 Bid / 1.55 Ask as of December 28, 2010 with the shares quoted at $7.11. If you owned the Calls at a profit and wished to exit the position, you would be ill advised to sell at the market Bid of 1.15. At this price, the option only carries $0.04 of extrinsic value ($0.04 = [6 +1.15] - $7.11) – this is a ridiculous Bid *as it assigns virtually no value for the additional 52 days left to expiration* (with a Delta not even close to 1). If you fired off the trade without putting the Call's market Bid premium into perspective, you would without a doubt be leaving money on the table. The key point: whatever the situation, it is always important to be cognizant of the make-up of the option premium you are either buying or selling.

4.2.7 "Moneyness"

An option can either be in-the-money, at-the-money or out-of-the-money. An in-the-money option has intrinsic value. Thus for a Call, an option is in-the-money if the Underlying stock price is greater than the Strike and for a Put if the Underlying stock price is less than the Strike. In Exhibit 4.7, the in-the-money options are the 45.0 and 46.0 Strike Calls and the 49.0 and 48.0 Strike Puts. The at-the-money options by market convention are the Strikes closest to the Underlying stock price (despite some existence of intrinsic value). In Exhibit 4.7, this would be the 47.0 Strike for the Calls and Puts. Finally, out-of-the-money options have no intrinsic value. Thus the 48.0 and 49.0 Strike Calls and the 46.0 and 45.0 Strike Puts in Exhibit 4.7 are the out-of-the-money options.

4.2.8 Time and Options

All options expire – because of this, the value of an option begins to decay the second it becomes available to trade. At expiration, the option will trade at Intrinsic Value (if any). For both option buyers and option sellers, it is thus very important to understand the impact of time on an option's value.

Exhibit 4.8 compares the difference between the July and November Series for EFG as of July 14, 2010. The July Series expires in 1 day and the November Series expires in 127 days. As you can clearly see, the difference between option premium values for the same Strike but different Series are dramatic.[33] For example, compare the July 45.0 Strike Put to the November 45.0 Strike Put. The July 45.0 Strike Put, with one day to expiration, is trading at 0.00 Bid / 0.02 Ask, basically worthless. The November 45.0 Strike Put, however with 127 days to expiration, is trading at 2.36 Bid / 2.40 Ask. This is a huge difference in value and demonstrates how the option premium (can potentially) erode for the benefit of the option seller at the expense of the option buyer.

Exhibit 4.8: Impact of Time on Options

Stock: EFG @ $47.26
Today: July 14, 2010
SERIES: JULY & NOVEMBER

CALLS					PUTS			
BID	ASK	Volume	O.I.	STRIKE	BID	ASK	Volume	O.I.
2.18	2.23	147	1,699	JUL 45.0	0.00	0.02	75	5,364
1.21	1.26	182	1,870	JUL 46.0	0.03	0.05	65	6,077
0.44	0.46	899	3,243	JUL 47.0	0.24	0.26	512	5,015
0.07	0.09	204	4,350	JUL 48.0	0.86	0.90	2,384	4,540
0.01	0.02	36	4,321	JUL 49.0	1.79	1.84	10	383
4.55	4.60	20	1,365	NOV 45.0	2.36	2.40	40	1,239
3.90	4.00	67	1,286	NOV 46.0	2.73	2.77	76	2,457
3.30	3.40	35	785	NOV 47.0	3.15	3.20	399	1,133
2.81	2.86	800	2,679	NOV 48.0	3.60	3.65	560	3,911
2.34	2.38	385	1,736	NOV 49.0	4.10	4.20	80	1,355

---

[33] This is a simple comparison and ignores other factors that impact option premium between Series, such as volatility.

4.3 THE FOUR FUNDAMENTAL OPTION POSITIONS

As mentioned earlier in the Chapter, at the most basic level, there are four fundamental option positions. One can be a Put Buyer, a Put Seller, a Call Buyer or a Call Seller – these are the four fundamental option positions. All option positions / strategies / structures, no matter how complex, emanate from these four positions. Do not be intimidated: if you gain an intuitive and deep understanding of the following four positions, you can understand *any* position / strategy / structure, no matter how "complex."

In this section, these four positions will be introduced using simple example trades for options on QRS stock, prices of which are located in Exhibit 4.9. In Chapter 6: Trade Structures, more complex positions will be introduced.

Exhibit 4.9: Option Chain for QRS Stock

Stock: QRS @ $37.12
Today: June 7, 2010
SERIES: DECEMBER

CALLS					PUTS			
BID	ASK	Volume	O.I.	STRIKE	BID	ASK	Volume	O.I.
4.90	5.00	58	337	DEC 36.0	4.25	4.35	56	1,616
4.35	4.45	180	161	DEC 37.0	4.70	4.80	173	1,254
3.85	3.95	160	229	DEC 38.0	5.20	5.30	160	1,657
3.40	3.50	276	551	DEC 39.0	5.75	5.85	39	2,310
2.98	3.05	103	3,016	DEC 40.0	6.30	6.40	15	3,492

4.3.1 Put Buyer

A Put Buyer is *bearish* on the Underlying stock. The Put Buyer therefore seeks to profit from a decline in the price of the Underlying.[34]

---

[34] Again, our initial focus will be on the *directional* movement of the Underlying (as opposed to changes in levels of volatility).

Key metrics for a Put Buyer:

Cost (Debit) = *(Premium x # Contracts x Multiplier)*
Maximum Risk = *(Premium x # Contracts x Multiplier)*
Break-Even[35] Price = *Strike Price – Premium*
(Bid/Ask) Spread Cost[36] = *[(Bid – Ask)]/2 x # Contracts x Multiplier*
Target Net Profit = *(Strike Price – Premium – Target Price) x*
#Contracts x Multiplier

Here is the Put Buyer example trade (refer to Exhibit 4.9 for option price quotes):

Buy 10 DEC 37.0 Put @ 4.80

Cost (Debit) = *(4.80 x 10 x 100) = $4,800*
Maximum Risk = *(4.80 x 10 x 100) = $4,800*
Break-Even Price = *37.0 – 4.80 = $32.20*
(Bid/Ask) Spread Cost = *[(4.80 – 4.70)/2] x 10 x 100 = $50*
Target Net Profit = *(37.0 – 4.80 - $27) x 10 x 100 = $5,200*

This trade costs $4,800 excluding commissions. Since we are a *buyer*, this $4,800 represents our maximum risk, i.e. the total amount of money we can potentially lose no matter what happens. In order to profit from this trade, we need the price of QRS in the example to drop below $32.20, the break-even price, by expiration. The Bid/Ask cost for this trade is $50. To determine a Target Net Profit we first determine an (estimated) Target Price that we assume for this example to be $27.[37] Based on this Target Price, the estimated Target Net Profit is $5,200. Exhibit 4.10 displays the P&L diagram at expiration for the Put Buyer.

---

[35] Break-Even defined as where profit and loss equals zero. Break-Even is the price where the Underlying stock needs to trade prior to Expiration for the trade to achieve zero profit.

[36] Assumes Broker uses mid-point basis of Bid/Ask for valuation of option position.

[37] Target Price can be estimated using technical or fundamental analysis, analyst price estimates or option implied price movements (to be discussed in Section 5.7).

Exhibit 4.10: Put Buyer P&L Diagram (at expiration)

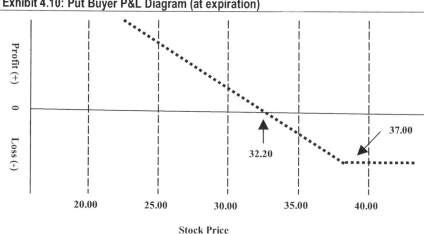

4.3.2 Put Seller

A Put Seller is **neutral to bullish** on the Underlying stock. A Put Seller therefore seeks to profit from *either no change or an increase* in the price of the Underlying.

Key metrics for a Put Seller:

Proceeds (Credit)   = *(Premium x # Contracts x Multiplier)*
Maximum Risk (theoretical)   = *(Strike – Premium – $0) x # Contracts x Multiplier*
Break-Even[38] Price   = *Strike Price – Premium*
(Bid/Ask) Spread Cost   = *[(Bid – Ask)]/2 x # Contracts x Multiplier*
Maximum Profit   = *(Premium x # Contracts x Multiplier)*

---

[38] Break-Even defined as where profit and loss equals zero.

72

Here is the Put Seller example trade:

Sell 15 DEC 36.0 Put @ 4.25

Proceeds (Credit)	$=(4.25 \times 15 \times 100) = \$6,375$
Maximum Risk (theoretical)	$= (36.0 - 4.25 - \$0) \times 15 \times 100 =$ $\$47,625$
Break-Even Price	$= 36.0 - 4.25 = \$31.75$
(Bid/Ask) Spread Cost	$= [(4.35 - 4.25)]/2 \times 15 \times 100 = \$75$
Maximum Profit	$= (4.25 \times 15 \times 100) = \$6,375$

Exhibit 4.11: Put Seller P&L Diagram (at expiration)

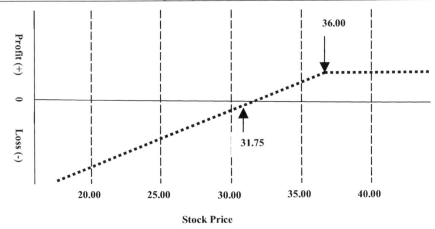

This trade brings in proceeds of $6,375 excluding commissions – yes, that is correct, you collect $6,375 in cash *up-front*. However, since you are a Seller, your maximum risk is undefined. In this example, your maximum risk is *theoretically* a total loss of $47,625 should QRS trade to zero by expiration – this is highly unlikely over the time horizon of the option but it demonstrates the potential risk. The Bid/Ask spread cost for this trade is $75. In order to profit from this trade, we need the price of QRS in the example to stay above $31.75, the break-even price, by expiration. Since we are a seller, the maximum profit for this trade is known and equivalent to the proceeds of $6,375. Exhibit 4.11 displays the P&L diagram at expiration for the Put Seller.

4.3.3 Call Buyer

A Call Buyer is **Bullish** on the Underlying stock. A Call Buyer therefore seeks to profit from an *increase* in the price of the Underlying.

Key metrics for a Call Buyer:

Cost (Debit)	*= (Premium x # Contracts x Multiplier)*
Maximum Risk	*= (Premium x # Contracts x Multiplier)*
Break-Even Price	*= Strike Price + Premium*
(Bid/Ask) Spread Cost	*= [(Bid – Ask)]/2 x # Contracts x Multiplier*
Target Net Profit	*= (Target Price – [Strike +Premium]) x #*
	Contracts x Multiplier

Here is the Call Buyer example trade:

Buy 20 DEC 40.0 Call @ 3.05

Cost (Debit)	*= (3.05 x 20 x 100) = $6,100*
Maximum Risk	*= (3.05 x 20 x 100) = $6,100*
Break-Even Price	*= 40.0 + 3.05 = $43.05*
(Bid/Ask) Spread Cost	*= [(3.05 – 2.98)/2] x 20 x 100 = $70*
Target Net Profit	*= ($45.0 – [40.0 +3.05]) x 20 x 100 = $3,900*

This trade costs $6,100 excluding commissions. Again, since we are a *buyer*, this $6,100 represents our maximum risk, i.e. the total amount of money we can potentially lose no matter what happens. In order to profit from this trade, we need the price of QRS in the example to increase above $43.05, the break-even price, by expiration. The Bid/Ask spread cost for this trade is $70. To determine a Target Net Profit we assume that QRS will increase to $45. Based on this price, the estimated or Target Net Profit is $3,900. Exhibit 4.12 displays the P&L diagram at expiration for the Call Buyer.

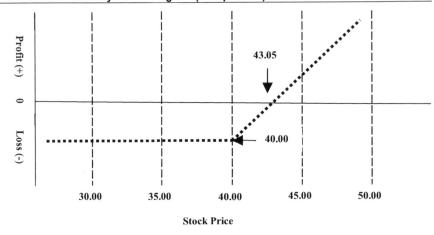

4.3.4 Call Seller

A Call Seller is **neutral to bearish** on the Underlying stock. A Call Seller therefore seeks to profit from *either no change or a decrease* in the Underlying.

Key metrics for the Call Seller:

Proceeds (Credit)	*= (Premium x # Contracts x Multiplier)*
Maximum Risk (theoretical)	*= Unlimited*
Break-Even Price	*= Strike Price + Premium*
(Bid/Ask) Spread Cost	*= [(Bid – Ask)]/2 x # Contracts x Multiplier*
Maximum Profit	*= (Premium x # Contracts x Multiplier)*

Here is the example trade for the Call Seller:

Sell 5 DEC 39.0 Call @ 3.40

Proceeds (Credit)	*= (3.40 x 5 x 100) = $1,700*
Maximum Risk (theoretical)	*= Unlimited*
Break-Even Price	*= 39.0 + 3.40 = $42.40*
(Bid/Ask) Spread Cost	*= [(3.50 – 3.40)]/2 x 5 x 100 = $25*
Maximum Profit	*= (3.40 x 5 x 100) = $1,700*

75

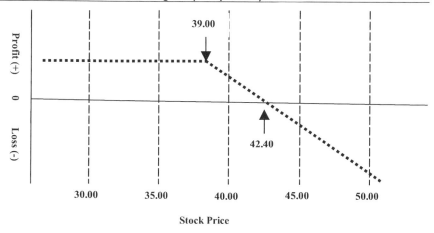

This trade brings in proceeds of $1,700 excluding commissions. However, since you are a Seller, your maximum risk is undefined and potentially unlimited – you are selling a Call which has theoretically no upside cap. In order to profit from this trade, we need the price of QRS in the example to stay below $42.40, the break-even price, by expiration. The Bid/Ask spread cost for this trade is $25. Since we are a seller, the maximum profit for this trade is known and equivalent to the proceeds of $1,700. Exhibit 4.13 displays the P&L diagram at expiration for the Call Seller.

4.4 BASIC OPTION VALUATION

4.4.1 Calculating Theoretical Value

Calculating the theoretical value of an option for retail trading purposes is quite easy. In such a situation the Black-Scholes model can be implemented – this option pricing model is the most basic and widely available. In order to calculate the theoretical value of the option using this model, we need several inputs. These include: the current date and expiration date of the option (to calculate the number of days left until expiration), the underlying stock price, the option strike price, the risk free rate, the dividend rate, whether it's a Put or Call and finally, the volatility estimate. Most brokerage websites will have an option pricing calculator; alternatively, you can use the option calculator at www.numa.com.[39] As an example, in Exhibit 4.14 we calculate the value of company XYZ's DEC 5.0 strike Call option.

Exhibit 4.14: Calculating XYZ 5.0 Call Theoretical Value

Inputs:	
Date:	Jun 15
Expiration:	Dec 15
Call Strike:	5.0
Stock price:	$2.50
Risk free rate (%)	1.0%
Dividend rate (%)	0.0%
Volatility:	150%
Output:	
Call Theoretical Value	0.58

In the above example, most of the inputs (such as the current date, expiration date, strike, stock price, Call or Put) are quite basic and self-explanatory. The risk free rate and the dividend rate inputs, for our purposes, will generally not factor significantly into the output (the theoretical value) given that the term of the options we will be active in are quite short, rates are (currently) low and small cap biotech stocks in general do not pay dividends. Thus the volatility estimate will be the key value that needs to be estimated. A basic approach is to "eye ball" a volatility estimate. Although this is a crude approach, it tends to work in practice for retail traders and does not require an advanced degree in mathematics. In order to "eye ball" a volatility estimate, you need to have access to at least a year's worth of volatility data (for both historic *and* implied volatility) displayed in chart format.

---

[39] www.numa.com/derivs/ref/calculat/option/calc-opa.htm.

Exhibit 4.15: XYZ Volatility Data Chart

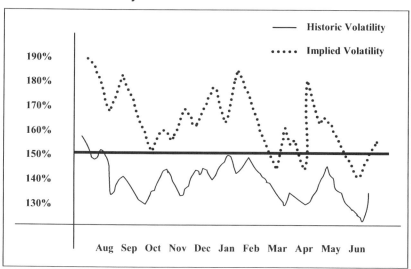

As mentioned, any good broker will have this data in their option trading technology offering. Historic volatility is the actual volatility *realized* by the underlying stock over the time period. The implied volatility is the volatility *implied* by the option premium over the time period. Implied volatility is normally higher than historic volatility. A good way to "eye ball" a volatility estimate is to simply look at a chart with both data points and find a middle value – very simple indeed. Looking at the volatility data in Exhibit 4.15, a good estimate would be around 150%. Next we plug the volatility estimate into the model and calculate the theoretical option value (the premium) of 0.58.

The aforementioned approach is useful for estimating the volatility (for the purpose of calculating theoretical value) under normal conditions. When a FDA or clinical trial catalyst is approaching or imminent, however, implied volatility is often several times greater than volatility under so-called normal conditions. In this situation, it is vital to evaluate the impact of changes in implied volatility on your option positions – this is discussed in Section 5.8: Scenario Testing.

4.4.2 (Non-Technical) Overview of the Greeks

Option traders use "the Greeks" to measure risk in their individual option positions and for their combined positions or portfolio. There are five Greeks employed to perform these functions: Delta, Gamma, Theta, Vega and Rho. The Greeks measure everything from how the option value will change with directional movement (i.e. up or down absolute dollar amounts) in the underlying (Delta), how the option value will change with an increase or decrease in the volatility of the underlying (Vega) and how the option value will change with the passing of time (Theta).[40] Gamma is a special Greek as it measures how the value of another Greek, the Delta, will change with the directional movement in the underlying.

Greeks are extremely important and it should be the goal of anyone wanting to trade or invest in options to gain an intuitive understanding of them – high-level math skills are not needed. An intuitive understanding of the Greeks will provide you with an understanding of the risk in your option position(s) and greatly contribute to your success as an option trader. This section seeks to provide a very simple, streamlined overview of the Greeks with the goal of giving the reader an intuitive understanding of the Greeks and their application. For this reason, do not view this section as a complete overview of the topic.

Delta

The Delta represents the amount the value of the option should change with a $1 move (up or down) in the underlying stock price. For example, if the Delta of the XYZ 5.0 Strike Call is 0.48 and XYZ stock moves down $1, then the value of the XYZ 5.0 Strike Call option *should* decline by $0.48. Alternatively, if

---

[40] Rho measures the impact of interest rates on the value of the option. This measurement is usually only used by institutional traders (trading in very large sizes) and will thus not be covered in this book.

XYZ stock moves up $1, then the value of the option *should* increase by $0.48. Delta basically means "Change." The reason I say "should" change is because many factors influence the value of an option and therefore the amount of change could deviate substantially based on other factors such as change in volatility, for example. Let's do some more examples – assume the following:

XYZ initial stock price = $20.17
XYZ 21 Strike Call 0.85 Bid/1.05 Ask (mid-point = (0.85+1.05)/2 = 0.95)
XYZ 21 Strike Call Delta = 0.43

XYZ Price	Change ($)	Delta	Call Value *(after $ change)*
$21.17	+$1.00	0.43	1.38 [= {0.43 x $1.00} + 0.95]
$19.17	($1.00)	0.43	0.52 [= {0.43 x ($1.00)} + 0.95]
$21.68	+$0.51	0.43	1.17 [= {0.43 x $0.51} + 0.95]
$21.00	($0.17)	0.43	0.88 [= {0.43 x ($0.17)} + 0.95]

If stock XYZ sells off by $1, from $20.17 to $19.17, the XYZ 21.0 Strike Call's value should decrease by 0.43, the amount of the Delta. Therefore, after this drop, the Call option value should change from 0.95 to 0.52 (= {0.43 x ($1.00)} + 0.95). The example above relates to Calls. What about Puts? The Delta for a Put is negative (note that the Delta for a Call is positive).[41] The calculations are basically the same:

XYZ initial stock price = $20.17
XYZ 21 Strike Put 1.65 Bid / 1.95 Ask (mid-point = (1.65+1.95)/2 = 1.80)
XYZ 21 Strike Put Delta = (0.57) ("( )" represent a negative number)

XYZ Price	Change ($)	Delta	Put Value *(after $ change)*
$21.17	+$1.00	(0.57)	1.23 [= {(0.57) x $1.00} + 1.80]
$19.17	($1.00)	(0.57)	2.37 [= {(0.57) x ($1.00)} + 1.80]
$21.68	+$0.51	(0.57)	1.51 [= {(0.57) x $0.51} + 1.80]
$21.00	($0.17)	(0.57)	1.90 [= {(0.57) x ($0.17)} + 1.80]

---

[41] The absolute value of the Deltas of a Call and Put of the same strike price should sum to 1. For example, the 21.0 Strike Call's Delta is 0.43. The 21.0 Strike Put's Delta is (0.57). Take the absolute value of each and they sum to 1 (= ABS[0.43 + (0.57)]).

Once again, it is important to note that Delta is only a guide to the *approximate* change of the value of the option with the directional change in the underlying – thus do not view this metric as the law.

Call Deltas range between 0.00 and 1.00 and Put Deltas range between (0.00) and (1.00) – that's it, Delta values cannot deviate outside of these values (i.e. there is no such thing as a Delta of, for example, 138). A Delta of 1.00 means the option's value changes exactly in-line with changes in the underlying stock (a deep in-the-money option). Likewise, a Delta of 0.00 means the option's value doesn't change at all with the changes in the underlying stock (a deep out-of-the-money option). An option with a Delta of 0.50 (or 50) is an at-the-money option. Often you will see or hear Deltas referred to in non-decimal format and/or also excluding a negative or positive value qualifier, i.e. a Delta of 43 (for the Call) or a Delta of 57 (for the Put). This is basically the same thing as expressed in decimal format with qualifiers and is said as shorthand by traders as the actual meaning is understood.

Gamma

Gamma simply represents the change of the Delta for a given change in the underlying stock – it is basically the "Delta of the Delta." For example, if the Delta of a Call is 0.50 (and the Call is worth, for example, 1.25) and Delta's Gamma is 0.05 and the underlying stock moves up $1.00, the Delta should change from 0.50 to 0.55 (= 0.50 + 0.05) following this move in the stock. So, based on this example, the value of this Call, from this $1 increase in the underlying stock, will change by 0.50 or from 1.25 to 1.75 (= 1.25 + 0.50). At this point in time, the Call's Delta is now 0.55. If the stock moves again by $1, it should therefore change the value of the option by $0.55.

Gamma basically shows the *potential* for your option position to "move" (in terms of value). For example, a "big Gamma" position can potentially experience explosive changes in value (and likewise the opposite for a small Gamma position). Additionally, it is important to note that Gamma can be either positive or negative. On that front, here are a few basic rules about Gamma to commit to memory:

*Long Calls and Long Puts have **positive** Gamma*
*Short Calls and Short Puts have **negative** Gamma*

Positive Gamma is generally good for your position and negative Gamma is generally bad for your position. For example, as the stock moves up and you are long a Call, positive Gamma will generate positive Deltas at an *increasing rate*. Likewise, if the stock moves down and you are long a Call, positive Gamma will generate negative Deltas at a *declining rate*. This is the magic of positive gamma. Confused? Let's use an example to demonstrate. Assume the following:

ABC Stock price = $30.00
Long ABC FEB 30.0 Call @ 2.00
Delta = 0.45
Gamma = 0.07

Exhibit 4.16: Positive and Negative Gamma

Price	Premium	Delta	Gamma	Implied Position*	
				Shares	Option
$27	0.82	0.30	0.04	45	30
$28	1.16	0.34	0.05	45	34
$29	1.55	0.39	0.06	45	39
$30	2.00	0.45	0.07	45	45
$31	2.45	0.52	0.06	45	52
$32	2.92	0.57	0.05	45	57
$33	3.49	0.61	0.04	45	61

* Initial share position represents 1 Call (= 1 x 100 x 0.45).

At the $30 starting point above, the long Call has a Delta of 0.45 – this is equivalent to being long 45 shares. As the price of ABC stock increases, the

Delta increases by the Gamma and the implied long share position increases at an increasing rate (please refer to the "Implied Position" column). Likewise, as the price of ABC stock decreases, the Delta decreases by the Gamma and the implied long share position decreases at a decreasing rate. In both situations, positive Gamma works to benefit your position: when the stock increases, your position increases (acting as sort of a "value enhancer"); when the stock decreases, your position decreases (acting as sort of a "speed break" to value destruction). The same situation holds for long Put but in reverse (i.e. when the stock decreases, your position increases; when the stock increases, your position decreases).

This brings us to negative Gamma. Negative Gamma is (as expected) the opposite of positive Gamma. A short Call or short Put is a negative Gamma position. So, assume in Exhibit 4.16 you are short the Call. In this situation, you are short an equivalent 45 shares. As the price of ABC stock increases, the short Delta increases by the Gamma and the implied short share position increases at an increasing rate – you are getting an increasingly large short position as the stock rises! Likewise, as ABC stock decreases, the short Delta decreases by Gamma at a declining rate and the short share position decreases at decreasing rate – your short position is getting increasingly smaller as the stock declines! This is negative Gamma. This situation is the same (in an opposite manner) for a short Put position. As you can see, it is vital to understand the Gamma in your position: ignore at your own peril.

Theta

Theta is very easy to understand: it measures the theoretical daily decay of the option premium assuming no changes in the stock price and volatility. The life of an option is finite with a defined expiration and therefore every day it decays in value – Theta measures this decay. Exhibit 4.17 shows the simple calculation for the impact of Theta on an option premium.

83

Exhibit 4.17: Theta Impact on Option Premium

Day	Stock	Option	Premium	Theta
Monday	ABC	JAN 12.0 Put	1.25	-0.05
Tuesday			1.20 (= 1.25 + -0.05)	
Thursday	XYZ	FEB 35.0 Call	2.50	-0.15
Friday			2.35 (= 2.50 + -0.15)	

Theta benefits option sellers and hurts option buyers. In the example above, the owner of the ABC JAN 12.0 Put "lost" $0.05 in premium for each option in 1 day – this $0.05 of premium went into the pocket of the individual who sold the option (the option seller). Likewise, the owner of the FEB 35.0 Call lost $0.15 in premium while the seller gained the same. **As mentioned, this is the theoretical amount of decay assuming no change in the stock price or volatility.**

An important concept to grasp with Theta is that it is not a constant amount (i.e. for the example, Theta decay does not stay at -0.05 or -0.15 for the life of the option). The more time an option has to expire, the smaller the impact of Theta. As the option begins to approach expiration, however, Theta begins to increase in a parabolic manner. The best way to demonstrate is through an example graph of Theta.

Exhibit 4.18: Graphical Depiction of the Impact of Theta over Time

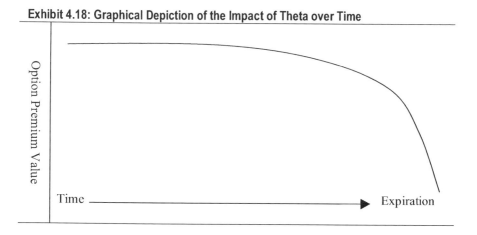

As Exhibit 4.18 shows, Theta is initially small and therefore the impact on the option premium is small. As the option approaches expiration, however, Theta rapidly increases, which causes the value of the option premium to lose value at an increasing rate – this concept is very important to understand for both option buyers and option sellers.

Vega

Vega measures the impact of a 1.00% change in volatility on the theoretical value of an option. For example, assume the ABC JUN 35.0 Call is priced at 1.50, the volatility of ABC stock is 27% and the ABC JUN 35.0 Call has a Vega of 0.23. If volatility increases by 1.0% to 28%, the Call price should increase from 1.50 to 1.73 (= 1.53 + 0.23). Likewise, if volatility decreases by 1.0% to 26%, the Call price should decrease from 1.50 to 1.27 (= 1.50 – 0.23). It is important to monitor your position Vega especially within the context of small cap biotech where changes in volatility are quite dramatic and violent.

PART II

CHAPTER 5.0

TRADING STRATEGY & TACTICS

5.1 OVERVIEW

Following a FRS assessment, you should have a basic understanding of the company's fundamental strengths and weaknesses. You should know the time horizon for the FDA or clinical trial catalyst event and have an idea of technical price levels. The next step is to translate this assessment into an actionable trade idea. Prior to discussing option trading structures, however, it is important to review a few notes on trading strategy and tactics. A well-planned, well-executed trade strategy will minimize your losses where you are wrong and maximize your profits where you are right.

5.2 PRE-TRADE ASSESSMENT

The first step is to take a very quick look at the company's option chains. Assess the availability of different expiration months, the number of available strikes, the level of open interest for each strike and the Bid / Ask spread for the different series of options. In some cases, trading the options simply does not make sense. It is usually a good idea to avoid trading the options of a stock if there are only one or two expiration months, only a few strikes available, limited open interest and high Bid / Ask spreads – this should be fairly obvious.

Exhibit 5.1: When to Avoid Trading Illiquid Options

< 2 Expiration months

< 3 Strikes available

< ~500 total contracts in open interest

   (for all strikes, months, for both Calls and Puts)

Premium spread > ~25% where premium spread = (Ask – Bid) / Strike

---

Trading into these situations is too costly and fraught with execution risk. Often a stock's options will exhibit a few but not all of these traits. In such situations you need to use a bit of discretion.

5.3 NO OPTIONS? NO STRIKES? NO PROBLEM

If you are very active trading options in the small cap biotech space you will more often than not run into the situation where options are either not traded on a specific company or where certain strikes in a company's option chains are not available. It may surprise you, but under this scenario it is possible to call the exchange to request the initiation of options on a company or the availability of specific strikes. You don't need to be a major fund or national broker to make these requests (although it helps). Yes, option exchanges are looking out for the proverbial little guy. Under this situation, I usually call the Chicago Board Options Exchange (the CBOE) at +1 (877) 843-2263 (check their website, cboe.com if the number is out of date). Follow the automated system and eventually you will reach a live person. For strikes, you simply need to state the name of the company, the ticker, the strike and the series. For example, I recently called to request the availability of the MannKind February 14.0 strike Call (strikes 1.0 through 15.0 were available with the exception of the 14.0). The CBOE individual will request your contact details (i.e. your phone number). They will take your request and then call you either that day or the next day to provide a response to the request (i.e. yes or no – they need to determine if there is market maker demand for said strikes) and when the strike will be available. Requesting the initiation of options on a company is (significantly) more difficult as basic criteria (such as minimum price, volume, etc.) as well as market demand need to be met. The live person at the CBOE will often provide an immediate response with respect to these requests and can answer any other questions you may have.

5.4 "LEGGING" IN

Legging in refers to constructing a multi-leg position in parts instead of filling the order's component parts at one price simultaneously with your broker. Legging in is most common for Call/Put spreads and butterflies. Legging in is best applied to companies where the stock has been trading in well-defined ranges or channels. For example, if you purchased 10 NOV 7.5/10.0/12.5 butterfly on XYZ stock with your broker in Exhibit 5.2 at market prices via a Limit Order, you would put in an order for and be filled at the following:

BUY 10 NOV 7.5 Call @ 1.55 = $1,550 (= 10*100*1.55)
SELL 20 NOV 10.0 Call @ 0.90 = ($1,800)[42] (= (20)*100*0.90)
BUY 10 NOV 12.5 Call @ 0.65 = $650 (= 10*100*0.65)

Total Amount Paid = $400
Price per Butterfly = $0.40

Exhibit 5.2: XYZ Call Option Quotes

Assumptions:
Date: May 15
Stock @ $6.50
Volatility: 100%

Call Bid	Call Ask	Strike
1.45	1.55	NOV 7.5
0.90	1.00	NOV 10.0
0.55	0.65	NOV 12.5

---

[42] ( ) denotes a credit, i.e. you sold the contracts and received the option premium in cash.

In this case, you placed an order for the butterfly and were filled. As this was a Limit Order (i.e. not a Market Order) there was no risk in the execution of your trade aside from it not being filled. As an aside, you should always place a Limit Order – NEVER place a Market Order when trading illiquid options (if you do, you will immediately know what it feels like to get ripped off).

Often, it is possible to trade into a position at a credit or at little to no cost. This is the theory behind legging into a trade. Of course, with the targeted lower to no cost for the position, the execution risk is increased and in some cases, the risk is increased substantially. Suppose you intend to do the aforementioned butterfly trade but instead wish to leg in. Below, we assume two simple scenarios:

Scenario A: XYZ stock increases $1.00 over duration of leg-in:

In this scenario, you buy 10 NOV 7.5 Call @ 1.55. The stock price increases by $1.00. The value of the Calls increase across the chain. The value of the NOV 10.0 strike Call is now 1.40 and the value of the NOV 12.5 Call is now 0.95. You proceed to sell 20 NOV 10.0 strike Call @ 1.40 and buy 10.0 NOV 12.5 strike Call @ 0.95. The total trade gives you a credit of 0.30, or $300. You are now basically being paid to do this trade – it is free and you will make at least $300 no matter what happens. If the stock ends up at the mid-point for the butterfly, i.e. the NOV 10.0 strike, you will achieve maximum value, or in this case around $2,800. If you do this for 100 butterflies (i.e. 100 NOV 7.5/200 NOV 10.0/100 NOV 12.5), that would be $28,000 risk free (after the trade leg-in). Not bad.

Exhibit 5.3: Scenario A – Increase by $1

Position Steps	Value @ +$1	Calculation	P&L
1. Initial Position			
NOV 7.5 CALL @ 1.55		1.55 * 10 * 100 =	1,550
2. Leg-In Position			
NOV 10.0 CALL @ 0.90	1.40	1.40 * (20) * 100 =	(2,800)
NOV 12.5 CALL @ 0.65	0.95	0.95 * 10 * 100 =	950
		CREDIT =	(300)

Scenario B: XYZ stock decreases $1.00 over duration of leg-in:

…Not bad until you consider the alternative scenario. In this scenario, you buy 10 NOV 7.5 Call @ 1.55. The stock price decreases by $1.00. The value of the Calls decrease across the chain. The value of the NOV 10.0 strike Call is now 0.59 and the value of the NOV 12.5 Call is now 0.35. Now the trade costs 0.72 or $720. You may decide not to do this trade at this point. In addition, your NOV 7.5 strike Calls are now worth 0.99, a loss of 0.56, or $560. At this juncture the original strategy to leg in is now in question and decisions will need to be made whether or not you close the position out at a loss, hold, or do some other strategic adjustment (such as, for example, selling the NOV 10.0 Call).

Exhibit 5.4: Scenario B – Decrease by $1

Position Steps	Value @ ($1)	Calculation	P&L
1. Initial Position			
NOV 7.5 CALL @ 1.55		1.55 * 10 * 100 =	1,550
2. Leg-In Position			
NOV 10.0 CALL @ 0.90	0.59	0.59 * (20) * 100 =	(1,180)
NOV 12.5 CALL @ 0.65	0.35	0.35 * 10 * 100 =	350
		DEBIT =	720

Based on this simple example, legging in can either be highly lucrative or very costly. For these reasons, several rules should be followed, for the more risk-averse trader, should you decide to leg in. First of all, NEVER leg into a position where the catalyst announcement is imminent (and unknown). Emphasis should be added to legging in where the initial leg-in is on the short side. For example, if you leg into a long Call butterfly position, and you initiate the trade by selling the body, in our example the NOV 10.0 Calls, and the Phase III is announced with positive results, you could be wiped out. If you need to leg in, always leg in on the long side.

For long butterfly positions, a good idea is to initiate the trade with an equal contract spread trade. In our example above, this would involve buying 10 NOV 7.5 Call @ 1.55 and selling 10 NOV 10.0 Call @ 0.90 for 0.65 or $650. In this case, you decrease your total risk by nearly 60% (1.55 debit versus 0.65 debit) if the stock drops to $0. If the stock increases by $1.00, as in our example, next *sell* the NOV 10.0/12.5 Call spread in equal contracts. In our example this would be to Sell 10 NOV 10.0 Call @ 1.40, Buy 10 NOV 12.5 Call @ 0.95 for a credit of 0.45 or $450. The net result is a butterfly that costs 0.20 or $200. Not as good as the credit or free trade but also not as risky. Of course you could always pay the original $400 to simultaneously fill the trade with your broker.

5.5 BUILD POSITIONS IN SMALL BLOCKS

The smaller the size of the trade, the easier and faster to fill the trade. This is one of the key "edges" afforded to the non-institutional trader versus the large institutional traders who must trade "in size" (which are usually filled by institutional brokers with large banks). This makes your trading more nimble and should get you better prices. You should exploit this element to every extent possible when you trade. For longer term positions (i.e. where the catalyst event is more than 6 months away), where liquidity is lower, this point cannot be emphasized enough – build positions slowly and in smaller blocks. Do not concern yourself with commissions. Commissions are now extremely low, and should no longer factor into or impact your decision to trade. A round trip commission should be immaterial to the overall value of the trade. If it is not, it is time to change your broker.

5.6   NEVER TRADE AT THE BID OR ASK

Never trade at the market Bid or Ask. This is especially true for illiquid option markets such as those found in small cap biotech. In liquid markets, such as SPY, where the Bid / Ask spread is .01, you obviously need to trade at the Bid / Ask. In small cap biotech, however, spreads can be as wide as 0.50 if not much wider. For example, Nabi Biopharmaceutical's (Ticker: NABI) June 7.5 Call was quoted at 0.30 / 0.75. This means that if I buy 10 of the Calls at the Ask it will cost me $750 (= 0.75 * 10 * 100). The value shown in my account will immediately show a loss of $225 on the trade (if the brokerage takes the mid-point value of the option, as discussed in Section 4.2.3: The Importance of Understanding The Bid/Ask Spread). If I for some reason want to get immediately out of the trade, I will have to sell at the Bid (0.30) and take an overall loss on the position of $450. This is not good.

An alternative route to selling or buying at the market Ask or Bid is to employ the following procedure:

   A.   First determine the theoretical value of the option(s).[43] The easiest way
        to do this is to use the Black-Scholes model (or other model) to
        calculate what the theoretical value should approximately be. Using
        my inputs (for the NABI Call options just discussed) I get a value of
        about 0.60 (see Section 4.4.1: Calculating Theoretical Value).
   B.   Next take the average of the current Bid / Ask which equates to 0.53 (=
        (0.30 +0.75) / 2)

---

[43] This step, i.e. determining the theoretical value of the option using Black-Scholes, is generally only needed for extremely wide Bid/Ask situations (greater than 0.50).

C. Compare the theoretical value of 0.60 and the average value of 0.53 to the Ask of 0.75.

Based on the data here, a trade should be possible in the range of 0.53 to 0.60 (probably 0.55). You may need to increase the amount to 0.65 that will undoubtedly get filled.

A good general strategy when trading in illiquid option markets is to initiate the trade at the average price of the Bid and Ask (highly annoying to market makers especially when the size is smaller). Hence, the NABI trade could have been initiated at 0.55. Do this for all trades including spreads and more complex trades. For example, if you are trading a long Call spread, take the average of both legs and subtract to get your initial spread value. If you are trading the XYZ 5.0 / 7.5 strike long Call spread (i.e. long the 5.0 Call, short the 7.5 Call) and the 5.0 Call is trading at 1.10 / 1.60 and the 7.5 Call is trading at 0.50 / 0.95, you would take the average of each strike, 1.35 for the 5.0 Call and 0.73 for the 7.5 Call. Next subtract both (since it is a long Call spread) to get 0.62. Round up to 0.65 and use this value as your *starting point* for the trade. You may often get filled at this value and when you are, the P&L impact on your portfolio is nearly zero. If this is the case, and you are building a larger position as already discussed, your next block order should be at a lower value. If you are not filled, you may need to slowly add increments of 0.05 or lower to the initial value. If you are not filled after several increments, cancel the order.

5.7 ESTIMATING PRICE MOVEMENT

Price movement can often be accurately estimated by looking at the at-the-money ("ATM") straddle of the month where the catalyst event is expected.[44] For example, stock XYZ is currently trading at $7.50 per share. Phase III

---

[44] For those inexperienced option traders, a straddle is a strategy where you would buy a Call and a Put at the same strike (a long straddle) or sell a Call and a Put at the same strike (a short straddle).

pivotal announcements are due in early November. The NOV 7.5 Call (mid-point) is trading at 3.20 and the NOV 7.5 Put (mid-point) is trading at 2.75. If we add the Call premium and the Put premium we get 5.95 (= 2.75 + 3.20). Now we subtract and add the total premium value to the current share price to get $1.55 and $13.54. This value range represents where the market is collectively predicting the price to move for both negative and positive outcomes. Based on experience, these estimates are often accurate and can provide you with a guideline where to structure your trade. The movement implied by option prices rarely lie.

5.8   SCENARIO TESTING

Prior to initiating a trade, you should always run a series of scenario analysis where you can determine maximum profit (and at what level), maximum loss (and at what level), overall profit structure (i.e. how the profit/loss diagram changes from maximum loss to maximum profit levels), how the P&L of the position develops/changes over time, and how the position is impacted by changes in implied volatility. You should _never_ initiate a trade unless you know this information. As mentioned, most brokerages will provide you with these tools – if your brokerage does not, you need to change your broker without delay.

In general, it is better to focus on maximum loss (your "risk") when running scenarios. For small cap biotech, as far as I am concerned, risk should always be defined and not open-ended. That is, it is generally a bad idea to have un-hedged short positions such as naked Calls. Naked Puts are generally ok given that most small cap biotech trades under $10 thus limiting downside with a "free" zero strike Put. Many argue, often correctly, that selling out of the money calls is very lucrative given the unlikely event of the price rallying x dollars. This may generally be true, but all it takes is one outlier to cause severe financial damage.

Defining profit and loss zones is (usually) straightforward – what is often overlooked in the scenario testing phase, however, is the impact from the collapse of implied volatility (often noted short hand as "IV") on your position. Usually prior to the catalyst event, implied volatility will likely be greater than 250%. Exhibit 5.5 graphically shows a typical volatility chart prior to a Phase III catalyst event. Immediately after the event, implied volatility will collapse, often substantially, regardless of an upward or downward move in the underlying stock. This can lead to unexpected and uncomfortable results for the uninitiated. For example, suppose stock XYZ trades at $8.50 prior to a Phase III announcement and an extremely bearish trader buys lots of 2.5 strike Put with implied volatility at 350% for $0.23 per option with one month to expiration.

Exhibit 5.5: Implied Volatility Pre-Catalyst Event

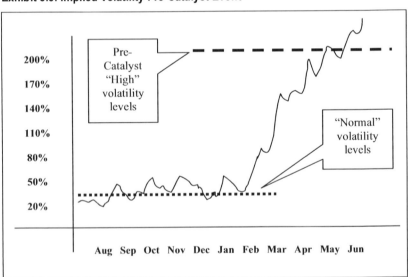

The trader is excited that he purchased such "cheap" options. The results come out and the stock plummets $6 to $2.50. The trader, excited, looks at his account and the position shows a near 40% loss. The reason, implied volatility drops from 350% to 50% (an extreme case) and the options now trade at $0.14.

Although this is a very simple example, it demonstrates the importance of monitoring the impact of changing implied volatility on your trading position – make sure you run this type of scenario prior to implementing a trade (achieved by changing the volatility estimate manually in the Black Scholes model as discussed or through your broker's option valuation software package). As a general guideline, the post-catalyst event volatility will often be a few notches below implied volatility that preceded the announcement by several months (represented by the "Normal" volatility level in Exhibit 5.5). Again, your broker should offer a tool that shows implied volatility levels graphically for at least a year in the past.

5.9 TAKE-OFF YOUR STOPS

With less than a month or so until a FDA or clinical trial catalyst event (or even after the event), it is always a good idea to take off your pre-set Stop Orders (for your stock holdings – never use Stop Orders with options). If you need to use a Stop Order, use a *mental* Stop Order (i.e. not an explicit order with your broker).

The key problem with a Stop Order is that it creates a "path of liquidity" for an individual or hedge fund that trades in size to "run the stops." It also makes you a victim of illegal bear raids (rarely enforced by the SEC) where naked short selling is used. Basically, a large player could come into the market and aggressively bid down the shares (often using naked shorting tactics, i.e. selling shares not borrowed or which do not exist) thus setting off all of the cumulative Stop (sell) Orders thus fueling an aggressive down spike in the share price which then allows the large player to buy into the selling thus pocketing the profits – dirty stuff and illegal although the SEC never seems to investigate these practices.

Probably the most recent legendary stop running/bear raid event in small cap biotech was with Dendreon.[45] The stock was trading in the high twenties following its successful Phase III results several weeks prior. The company was slated to make a high profile presentation related to the successful Phase III drug results at an important conference in April 2009. Several hours before the presentation at the conference, the shares plummeted from the high twenties to less than $8 a share in a few minutes prior to being halted. The next day, they traded back up to the high twenties. If you held the shares and had a Stop Order you would have had huge losses (depending on what Stop price was used) for no reason. There was no major investigation into the occurrences that day. The SEC was silent thus communicating to investors/traders that "you are on your own."

5.10 (VERY) HIGH SHORT INTEREST = DANGER

If you trade or invest in the small cap biotech space you will usually be exposed to companies with rather substantial short interest compared to companies outside of the industry – this comes with the territory. I consider a "normal" short interest in most FDA and clinical trial catalyst events to be in the range of 10% to 15% or a bit higher. When you are confronted with a short interest above 20% or even higher, an extra level of care and due diligence is highly advised if you are trading from a long (bullish) position. Short interest this high indicates big money, institutional short interest. Shares are likely very hard to borrow (should you wish to short) and borrow fees are likely very high as the shares are offered to the best clients (i.e. hedge funds, etc.) of institutional brokers. The point is simple: big money with substantial, well-funded research is betting against the bullish scenario. You need a very good reason to adopt a

---

[45] Dendreon's drop was largely attributed to naked short selling, however, the significant level of Stop Orders added a huge boost to the share plummet.

bullish stance in this situation. Often the big money is wrong – just be advised to take extra care when confronted with very high short interest.

5.11   MONITOR OPTION ACTIVITY PRE-CATALYST

When a company is within a few weeks of a catalyst event, it is very important to monitor, for the relevant expiration series, both option volumes and option open interest levels at available strike prices. The best way to do this, in my opinion, is to print out the option chains for the relevant expiration series at the end of each trading day and then compare to the following day (for a week to several weeks prior). Monitoring both volume and open interest can be very revealing and provide valuable insight in the final days preceding a catalyst event. To monitor volume, look at what strikes have the heaviest volume and which options, Calls or Puts, are the most active. This will generally provide some cursory indication of whether the market is bearish or bullish on the company's prospects (if you have followed the company for several weeks and initiated a position this knowledge should be second nature). To get a more detailed look at the order flow, however, you need to focus on *net* changes in open interest. To do this, compare the prior day's open interest levels to the (current) beginning of day open interest. For example, Exhibit 5.6 tracks the open interest in the AUG 5.0 strike Call options of Company XYZ.

Exhibit 5.6: Monitoring Net Changes in Open Interest

AUG 5.0 Call	Volume	Open Interest (BOD)	Net Change
Day 1 (open)	-0-	25,000	
Day 1 (close)	5,000		
Day 2 (open)	-0-	28,000	+3,000
Day 2 (close)	10,000		
Day 3 (open)	-0-	35,000	+7,000
Day 3 (close)	15,000		
Day 4 (open)	-0-	50,000	+15,000
Day 4 (close)	25,000		
Day 5 (open)	-0-	25,000	(25,000)

Comparing the day-to-day net change in open interest, it becomes clear that there is heavy, and increasingly large, accumulation at this strike (Day 2 +3,000, Day 3 +7,000 and Day 4 +15,000). On day 5, however, there is a significant reduction in open interest meaning a large portion of the options were closed out. This occurred the *day prior* when the strike experienced very high volume concentrated in one trade; some seeing the trade may have thought this was a huge bullish trade (thus presumably adding to open interest) made by an institutional trader which may have enticed them to put on a similar trade. The next day, however, open interest declined substantially. **Someone, somewhere, trading in size (and therefore presumably "in the know"), took profits and did not want to hold into the catalyst event.** If I am long the AUG 5.0 Call, and I saw this, I would seriously consider either exiting or taking some other risk hedging action, such as selling the AUG 7.5 Call. Of course, this example is simplified and analyzes only one strike – in reality, you need to look at all relevant strikes to see what is going on. The point is, it is very important and of value monitoring open interest when nearing a catalyst event as it gives you a picture of order flow and may foreshadow coming events.

5.12   EXIT OR HOLD PRE-CATALYST?

If you entered a trade early enough to generate decent profits you will be confronted with an important question: do you exit the position or do you hold into the announcement? The more P&L the trade has made prior to the announcement, the harder this decision may be. A good strategy (widely known as the "run up" method) adopted by many is to exit into (i.e. prior) the catalyst event. This approach may yield consistent although not spectacular profits. This decision will obviously depend on your personal situation and your risk tolerance. Usually, when faced with this decision, the best approach is to assess the profit under several scenarios: full exit, hold (with positive outcome), hold (with negative outcome, assume zero, i.e. full loss of all accrued profit plus trade original cost), or exit half/hold half. This will put values in perspective and will allow a more informed choice. If your profits are large and you have trouble sleeping or are extremely stressed, by all means you should exit: a profit is a lot easier to handle than a large loss. Of course if you exit and it turns out that the results were positive on your position, you will have a great deal of regret. Having traded awhile, I can say that I prefer regret (over losses of greater profits having already taken profits) to sadness (over losses and <u>no</u> profits) – the latter is harder to stomach. Generally the best approach is to take 50% profits and hold 50% into the results – then the feelings will even out!

5.13   EXIT POST CATALYST?

Prior to a catalyst event, you should always have a plan what you are going to do after the announcement for both positive and negative outcomes. For negative results (i.e. from the perspective of your trade) where you are net long, it is generally always a good idea to exit the position on the day of the announcement. This is primarily due to the fact that liquidity will be at its highest level, allowing you to exit at lower Bid / Ask spreads before liquidity substantially drops over the next several days. Although high short interest will require shorts to cover, thus driving the stock up over several days, the rise in the stock price, following a negative catalyst outcome, will generally not be enough to increase the option premium to compensate for the collapsing implied volatility. The point is, this is a failed trade, get out. If you don't get out, you will eventually have a dead money position that you cannot exit. For negative results where you are net short, get out after the first half hour. Do not hold onto the position and hope that it will move into your favor (because it probably won't).

For positive results where you are net long, the decision is usually more difficult. I generally prefer to exit after the first half hour (when the stock has stabilized and option Bid / Ask spreads have narrowed substantially). The reason is that the catalyst event has occurred, liquidity is at its height and volatility is collapsing. Also, the profit earned is not yet realized until you close out your position – the market can always take it back which would be a crushing blow. Generally the only time to hold onto a position after positive news is if the drug candidate is "blockbuster" in nature, that is, if it targets a disease where there is no effective treatment and thus could yield the company billions of dollars in future profits. In such a scenario, it is likely that the shares will rally over the following weeks given news on the company and increased interest from new investors. Also, the company could be a prime candidate for a buyout by a major pharmaceutical company that should also fuel share price appreciation (even if only on rumor). For positive results where you are net short, simply allow the short options to expire worthless or close them out.

5.14   GETTING OUT OF ILLIQUID (LONG) OPTION POSITIONS

In certain situations where you are long in-the-money options (for Puts and Calls) and have accrued decent profits you may want to exit the position (basically, you want to "book" your profits). In illiquid markets the wide Bid / Ask can often make this difficult and somewhat costly. Also, the quoted market Bid side is often below the intrinsic value of the stock (basically, the market maker is trapping you in the position and wants to extort free money from you to allow you out of the position) – I have been trading for a long time and this always seems to happen (and is highly annoying). For example, ABC is trading at $7.50 a share and a trader owns the 5.0 strike Calls. The trader has made decent profits on the position (buying when the shares were trading at $4.50 and the 5.0 strike Calls at 0.50) and wants to book profits. ABC is an illiquid stock and the 5.0 strike Calls are trading at 2.30 Bid / 2.65 Ask. The trader realizes this is a bad deal: the 5.0 strike Call Bid should be trading (or be able to be traded at) *at the very least* 2.50 ($7.50 – 5.0 strike = 2.50 versus a Bid of 2.30) – at 2.50 the option is Delta one and reflects no time value. Basically the trader is giving up 0.20 (= 2.50 – 2.30) of free money to the market maker. A good way to handle this frequently occurring situation (and to "stick it" to the market maker) **is to simply *exercise* the option**. Remember that the option buyer has the right, in this example, to buy ABC at $5 anytime up to expiration. By exercising the Calls, the trader gets ABC shares at $5 and can turn around and sell them at $7.50 (thus reaping the 0.20 additional upside not reflected in the option Bid quote minus a nominal exercise fee imposed by your broker). Before exercising, attention must be made on two elements. First, calculate the position combined P&L to see if it makes sense to exercise. In the example, the trader purchased the 5.0 strike Calls for 0.50 so it only makes sense to exercise where: current share price > premium paid + strike. Using the numbers in the example, we get: $7.50 > 0.50 + 5.0. So if the trader exercises, the individual buys the shares at $5.00 and sells them for $7.50. The profit on the trade is 2.00 (= 7.50 – 5.0 – 0.50). The second element that needs to be factored into a decision on whether or not to exercise is overnight risk. As a trader, you will notify your brokerage of your desire to exercise *the day before* (preferably near market close). Thus you take overnight risk converting your option to the actual shares. If the stock makes a big move, you can potentially lose more than the value of the original option (of course you could actually make more). Thus there is a risk that the operation will be less profitable than simply taking the unfavorable Bid "hit." For obvious reasons, care should be taken to not exercise prior to major catalyst announcements or other market moving info such as earnings announcements. Make sure you understand overnight risk prior to exercise.

For Puts, I suggest against using this exit strategy (although it is, of course, possible). In such a situation, you become *short* the stock which may expose you to significant and adverse upside risk (takeover?) and also hard to borrow fees or automatic buy in and associated fees and penalties (don't forget these are illiquid stocks). Although such situations are (very) rare, never underestimate the market's ability to crush you at the point you are the most exposed.

5.15 ESTIMATING PRICE ON FAILURE

It is always a good idea to assess the potential downside on a failed catalyst event. This knowledge can either be used to determine potential risk where you are long or determine potential profit where you are short. Estimating downside is often quite difficult given the numerous variables involved in a company's valuation (i.e. cash, ownership, pipeline, industry support). In such a situation one needs to use a bit of discretion. A good approach (and one used by most who actively trade small cap biotech) is to use cash per share as a *floor value* in a negative outcome scenario. This method is often most useful for companies with a single, late stage drug candidate (as there is no other immediate and tangible value aside from cash on the balance sheet left in the company on a failed event). Using this method is a bit more complicated where the company has multiple late stage candidates (or promising earlier stage candidates) and/or approved products. In these situations, use cash per share as a floor and add to it the additional value from the other candidates or products. Calculating this additional value is, obviously, quite difficult – a simple (and very crude) way is to use a prior year's technical price performance to "separate" the value of the other products/ candidates from the value of the failed late stage candidate. For example, XYZ is has a late stage drug candidate, several earlier stage candidates and one approved product. Also, the company has approximately $2.00 cash per share. Over the past six months, the company's shares have rallied to $6.00 on excitement of the late stage drug candidate. Prior to this run up, the shares traded in a range between $3.00 and $4.00. Based on this information, one could crudely estimate a price on failure by taking the cash per share ($2.00) and adding the "value" from the other candidates and products of $1.50 (= [$3.00 + $4.00]/2 - $2.00). A price on failure estimate would thus be around $3.50 (=

$2.00 + $1.50) – of course depending upon the exact situation, this could be either overly aggressive or overly optimistic.

5.16 THE SALVAGE VALUE STRATEGY

On a failed catalyst event it is often possible to extract value from a losing option position before the quote goes 0.00 Bid / 0.05 Ask. In these situations traders will often keep losing, near-term expiration positions while hoping for some "miracle" scenario to bail them out (such as an immediate buyout) – when the miracle does not materialize (almost 99.9% of the time), the trader is left with a phantom P&L position which will eventually show a loss when the options expire. For example, near the end of August, XYZ announced a failed Phase III before the open of the market. The stock was at $10 and a trader owns 40 SEP 12.0 strike Calls. The stock begins to trade pre-market (before options begin to trade) down $5 a share – this is clearly a massively failed event with limited potential to realize any value from the SEP 12.0 strike Calls. If the trader does nothing, the options will quickly trade to 0.00 Bid / 0.05 Ask – i.e. the trader is trapped in the position. Until the options expire, the trader will have $100 positive P&L value in their account assuming the brokerage uses a mid-value price convention (= 40 x [(0.00 + 0.05)/2] x 100). When the options finally expire in September, the person will begin the following week with a $100 loss. Fortunately, there is a salvage strategy that works most (but not all) of the time that I use in these situations (when option expiration is close; for further dated expirations such as more than 3 months, I may keep the position as the stock may rally during the ensuing months which often happens). Also, use of the salvage strategy is better for larger option positions (for 10 or fewer contract positions, the salvage value method does not really make sense when factoring in commissions). The salvage strategy works best when the news event occurs after-hours or pre-market (i.e. when option markets are closed) and where the stock makes an indicative move allowing one to assess the seriousness of the failed event. In such a situation (for Calls), immediately assess the impact and put in a Limit order to sell, **at market open**, your position at 0.05 – in extreme moves, the price at which you intend to sell is easy and is usually 0.05 – for closer situations (where the stock drop is not as big), I suggest the use of the option pricing model (with revised (lower) price and (lower) volatility estimates) to fine tune the amount which can often be greater than 0.10. If it is too close to call, it is often better to not use the salvage strategy and to simply see where the options open – the worst thing that can happen is to sell at too low of a value! On a recent (major) failed event, I managed to get 50 Calls out the door at the market open to realize $250 – after the sale, the option went immediately 0.00 Bid / 0.05 Ask (where it recently expired) – apologies to the guy (or gal) that bought these from me.

5.17   TRADING ADVISORY PANELS

One of the most interesting events in small cap biotech trading is the Advisory Panel. As mentioned in Chapter 1: Background, an Advisory Panel is a single day meeting where independent industry experts review and opine on a drug candidate's data presented by the company and FDA reviewers. At the end of the meeting a vote is taken by the committee to decide whether or not to approve the drug and under what conditions, if any. A positive committee vote normally bodes very well for the company's drug candidate whereas a negative vote can be quite damaging for the drug candidate's prospects. It is important to note that the FDA is not required to follow the recommendations of the Committee (but usually does). These events are usually broadcast live over the internet (via FDA-related feeds) and also "live blogged" by individuals in the media somewhat akin to a professional sporting event.

From a trading perspective, there are essentially three key periods during an Advisory Panel event: Briefing Document Release, Pre-Panel Interim Period (the period between the release of the briefing docs but before the Advisory Panel Day) and Advisory Panel Day. Each of these periods is discussed below:

Briefing Document Release

The Briefing Documents, referred to in short as the "Briefing Docs," outline the Panel's primary concerns, comments, questions and observations with regards to the drug or device candidate under review. The Briefing Docs are typically released around *two* days prior to the slated Advisory Panel date. Prior to the release of these documents, the market will maintain a general idea with regards to their contents. Any unexpected (either positive or negative) elements and or contents can produce substantial stock price movement (both up or down).

It is very difficult if not impossible to determine, in advance, how the market will react to the briefing docs. As such, it is often advantageous to err on the side of caution when trading these situations. For example, if you are long Calls, consider exiting your position entirely or consider some hedging operation if you have already accrued profits. Under the full exit scenario, you maintain the option to re-enter the position under both negative and neutral (i.e. in-line with market consensus) briefing docs. If you wish to maintain a long Call position, a potential hedging operation could be to sell higher strike Calls (thus producing a Call spread) into the release. Under this scenario, the sold higher strike Calls will offset some of the losses in a negative outcome. Similar actions should be taken for Put positions (i.e. if you are long Puts, consider selling a lower strike Put thus creating a Put spread). The point is, decide in advance what you intend to do (full exit, full hold, some hedging operation) prior to the release of these documents – don't ignore the potential this "news" can have on your position.

Pre-Panel Interim Period

The Pre-Panel Interim Period is usually two days in length and is a great time to prepare for the main event, the Advisory Panel Day. It is often a great time to exit and or adjust existing positions or to implement new positions. This interim period will often be defined by the nature of the briefing docs and the subsequent market reaction. Do not be fooled: nothing really matters until the Advisory Panel vote. Even under the most negative (or positive) scenario, the Panel may vote for approval (or denial) of the product candidate. A good example is with regards to MELA Sciences. The briefing docs were extremely negative and the shares dropped more than 50% on the release date. Everyone was saying the company was doomed. The Advisory Panel, however, voted for approval of the company's MelaFind Skin Cancer detection device and the shares rocketed up over 100%. Although ultimate approval may not be granted (remember the FDA still has final say on the matter) the jump in the stock price produced a decent trading opportunity. The point is you only have two days to prepare for the Advisory Panel (when the shares will be halted and you are unable to do anything).

Advisory Panel Day

During the Advisory Panel the stock is (almost always) halted. The Panel usually lasts the entire day with the vote at the end of the day. The voting will often occur near the close of market or the after-hours session. Following the vote, the company will decide whether or not to open the shares for trading. To check the status for NASDAQ listed stocks (where most small cap biotechs trade), go to www.nasdaqtrader.com and click on "Trading Halts" – if the shares are slated to open, the site will make note of it and list the time for the resumption of quotes and trading. Once the stock opens for trading, the market will render its final decision with regards to the company's drug candidate.

CHAPTER 6.0

TRADE STRUCTURES

6.1 OVERVIEW

In this section I present my favorite fifteen trade structures to use when trading small cap biotech FDA and clinical trial catalyst events. The trade structures range from very simple to more advanced. Each trade structure includes an example trade with associated assumptions. At the end of the section, I quickly review some trade structures for earlier stage companies and discuss trade structures that are not recommended for catalyst events. Examples for all trade structures are similar in nature to actual trades performed by the author over the past several years.

6.2 TRADE STRUCTURE REVIEW PRIMER

Each trade structure review is divided into six key sections that cover its application, the assumptions used for the example trade, the trade construct, position P&L (for the example trade), a risk diagram and commentary. Below I provide a brief description of how each section functions:

A. Application

This section covers the conditions where the trade structure is optimized (i.e. the conditions under which the trade structure will achieve optimal results). These are general guidelines and should therefore not disqualify using this structure where the conditions are not met. To simplify matters, conditions are framed in four categories: Time Horizon, Underlying Share Price, Sentiment and levels of Implied Volatility. Exhibit 6.1 lists these conditions and provides further granularity. Determining the "Sentiment" of the trade, i.e. whether or not to use a bullish, bearish or neutral structure is determined by your own analysis / external analysis (i.e. blogs, analysts) and / or by an optimal asymmetric risk / reward profile (to be discussed in Chapter 7.0)

Exhibit 6.1: List of Conditions

TIME HORIZON	SENTIMENT
< 1 month to Catalyst Event > 1 month < 6 months > 6 months	Bearish Bullish Neutral
UNDERLYING SHARE PRICE	VOLATILITY
Share price < $2.50 Share price > $2.50 < $7.50 Share price > $7.50	Under 200% > 200% < 350% > 350%

B. Assumptions

This section covers the assumptions for the trade example that is listed in the "Trade Construct" section (Part C, below). Assumptions include: the trade date, stock price, estimated catalyst date (date of announcement or news), implied volatility (for the options in the trade), expiration date (number of days until expiration of the options in the trade structure) and the price estimate for a positive and negative outcome of the catalyst event.

C. Trade Construct

This section demonstrates, in table format, how the trade is constructed. This section uses the data from the "Assumptions" sections in order to calculate the values of the option premium in the table using the Black-Scholes option pricing model. A "Buy" of a Call or Put option is denoted by a "B" followed by the number of contracts next to the premium paid (the "trade description"). For example, a Buy of 10 DEC 7.5 Call for 1.25 would be listed in the CALLS Column, under ASK, in the DEC 7.5 Row and listed in the cell as "[B10@1.25]." This is demonstrated in Exhibit 6.2. Likewise, a "Sell" of a Call or a Put option is denoted by an "S" followed by the number of contracts next to the premium received. For example, a Sell of 10 DEC 7.5 Put for 1.30 would be listed in the PUTS Column, under BID, in the DEC 7.5 Row listed in the cell as "[S10@1.30]." The premium amount followed by the trade description represents the Bid or Ask prior to the trade – it is assumed that a trade can be made somewhere between the Bid / Ask, as discussed in the chapter on Trading Strategy & Tactics. For example, "[S10@1.30]/1.25" under the PUTS, BID column, means that a trade was made at 1.30 despite the fact that the market Bid prior to the trade was 1.25.

Exhibit 6.2: Example of Trade Construct Notation

CALLS			PUTS	
BID	ASK	STRIKE	BID	ASK
		DEC 2.5		
		DEC 5.0		
1.20	[B10@1.25]/1.30	DEC 7.5	[S10@1.30]/1.25	1.35
		DEC 10.0		

D. P&L

This section shows the P&L of the trade including: the trade order, the initial cost (credit or debit), maximum profit (and associated price level(s)) and maximum loss (and associated price level(s)). It should be noted that profit and loss levels are based on theoretical assumptions that may or may not be currently achievable in actual market trading.

E. Risk Diagram

This section shows the approximate P&L diagram for the trade at various price levels. This diagram represents the P&L at expiration.

F. Commentary

This section provides trade structure specific comments where appropriate.

6.3 TRADE STRUCTURES

6.3.1 Leveraged Call (Un-Hedged)

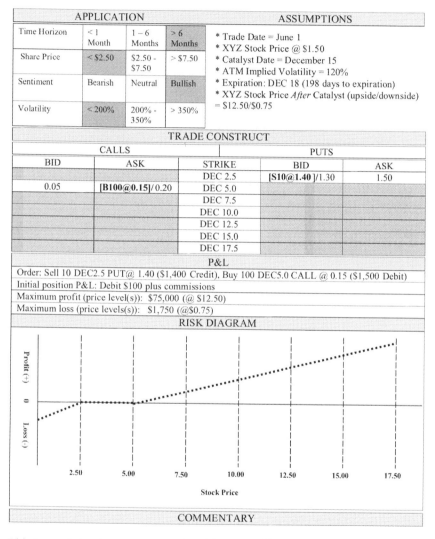

APPLICATION				ASSUMPTIONS
Time Horizon	< 1 Month	1 – 6 Months	> 6 Months	* Trade Date = June 1
Share Price	< $2.50	$2.50 - $7.50	> $7.50	* XYZ Stock Price @ $1.50 * Catalyst Date = December 15 * ATM Implied Volatility = 120%
Sentiment	Bearish	Neutral	Bullish	* Expiration: DEC 18 (198 days to expiration) * XYZ Stock Price *After* Catalyst (upside/downside)
Volatility	< 200%	200% - 350%	> 350%	= $12.50/$0.75

TRADE CONSTRUCT					
CALLS			PUTS		
BID	ASK	STRIKE	BID		ASK
		DEC 2.5	[S10@1.40]/1.30		1.50
0.05	[B100@0.15]/ 0.20	DEC 5.0			
		DEC 7.5			
		DEC 10.0			
		DEC 12.5			
		DEC 15.0			
		DEC 17.5			

P&L
Order: Sell 10 DEC2.5 PUT@ 1.40 ($1,400 Credit), Buy 100 DEC5.0 CALL @ 0.15 ($1,500 Debit)
Initial position P&L: Debit $100 plus commissions
Maximum profit (price level(s)): $75,000 (@ $12.50)
Maximum loss (price levels(s)): $1,750 (@$0.75)

RISK DIAGRAM

COMMENTARY

This type of structure represents the ultimate upside trade (and is thus very rare). Basically you have a low priced (< $2.50) small cap biotech stock with little institutional following and a major catalyst about six months or more away. In

114

this structure, it is vital to do your due diligence as you will be building and holding the trade for at least six months. For this trade, look for companies with low shares outstanding (< 50.0 million) and cash per share of > $1.00 (aside from product potential and other fundamental elements). It is often possible to find a company with cash per share greater than the share price – this represents a very good opportunity as the company is essentially valued at zero and your downside is theoretically buffeted by cash on the balance sheet. Be wary and treat with caution companies with very low cash and other poor fundamentals – in such circumstances, it may be good to avoid. In this structure (and based on this example), 5.0 strike Call options are frequently priced from 0.05 to 0.20 and illiquid.[46] However, they can be traded into at around 0.15 (often even lower at around 0.10) but it usually takes a few weeks to do so. As per the structure, 5.0 strike Call purchases are financed by selling 2.5 strike Puts (at a 10 to 1 ratio or as much as possible). The goal of the structure is to finance as many Calls with sold Puts in order to initiate the trade at the lowest possible cash outlay – in the example, we trade in at $100 debit. During the duration of the trade, the Put option you sold will generally offset the time decay of the Call options. When you are nearing the catalyst event, it is generally a good idea to take off (i.e. buy back) the Puts (normally at a profit). This will limit your downside in the event of a negative announcement. As word gets out about the impending catalyst, and as the actual announcement date nears, the share price will normally climb rapidly. At this juncture, you may have substantial profits and you will need to make a decision whether or not you will hold into the announcement. As previously discussed, at this juncture, it is important to run scenarios to make a well-informed decision regarding trade decisions. It may also be of value to structure a bearish trade (simultaneously with your existing long position) so you can benefit (or lessen your loss) should there be a negative result.

---

[46] This example specifically references the 5.0 strike Call. This structure of course applies to other low strikes (i.e. < 5.0).

6.3.2 Leveraged Call (Hedged)

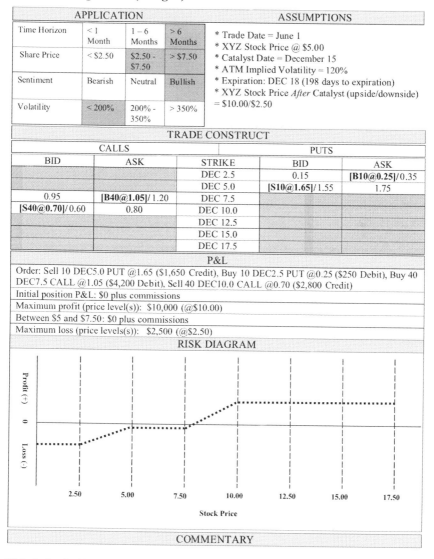

APPLICATION				ASSUMPTIONS
Time Horizon	< 1 Month	1 – 6 Months	> 6 Months	* Trade Date = June 1
Share Price	< $2.50	$2.50 - $7.50	> $7.50	* XYZ Stock Price @ $5.00 * Catalyst Date = December 15 * ATM Implied Volatility = 120%
Sentiment	Bearish	Neutral	Bullish	* Expiration: DEC 18 (198 days to expiration) * XYZ Stock Price *After* Catalyst (upside/downside)
Volatility	< 200%	200% - 350%	> 350%	= $10.00/$2.50

TRADE CONSTRUCT					
CALLS			PUTS		
BID	ASK	STRIKE	BID	ASK	
		DEC 2.5	0.15	[B10@0.25]/0.35	
		DEC 5.0	[S10@1.65]/1.55	1.75	
0.95	[B40@1.05]/1.20	DEC 7.5			
[S40@0.70]/0.60	0.80	DEC 10.0			
		DEC 12.5			
		DEC 15.0			
		DEC 17.5			

P&L
Order: Sell 10 DEC5.0 PUT @1.65 ($1,650 Credit), Buy 10 DEC2.5 PUT @0.25 ($250 Debit), Buy 40 DEC7.5 CALL @1.05 ($4,200 Debit), Sell 40 DEC10.0 CALL @0.70 ($2,800 Credit)
Initial position P&L: $0 plus commissions
Maximum profit (price level(s)): $10,000 (@$10.00)
Between $5 and $7.50: $0 plus commissions
Maximum loss (price levels(s)): $2,500 (@$2.50)

RISK DIAGRAM

COMMENTARY

This is basically the same trade as the "un-hedged" leveraged Call as discussed above except for the inclusion of the purchased lower strike Put (the "hedge") and the higher strike sold Call. This trade is structured to maximize gain and minimize loss for higher priced stock situations (where stock price is greater than $5). Inclusion of the hedge is obviously optional but, in my opinion, should always be a part of this structure in these situations for basic risk management – it is always advisable to define your downside prior to a major catalyst event; the hedge in this example provides this safety. Inclusion of the higher strike sold Call reduces your absolute risk (your capital outlay) at the expense of reducing your upside. In the above example, the capital outlay is zero due to the inclusion of the sold 10.0 strike Call – as thus, the structure is optimized. In the example above, the structure loses money between zero and the 5.0 strike Put (however, loses are capped at the 2.5 strike Put). The structure makes money above the 7.5 Call strike with maximum value attained above the 10.0 Call strike. The trade neither loses nor makes money between $5.00 and $7.50 given that the initial P&L is zero. A good variant of this structure (in terms of trade execution) is to initiate the trade without the higher strike sold Call several months in advance of the catalyst event. If the stock price increases later on (a good probability) then you retain the option to sell the higher strike Call (the 10.0 strike Call in this example) at a substantially higher premium, further reducing risk and enhancing profit potential.

6.3.3 (Long) Call and Put Spreads

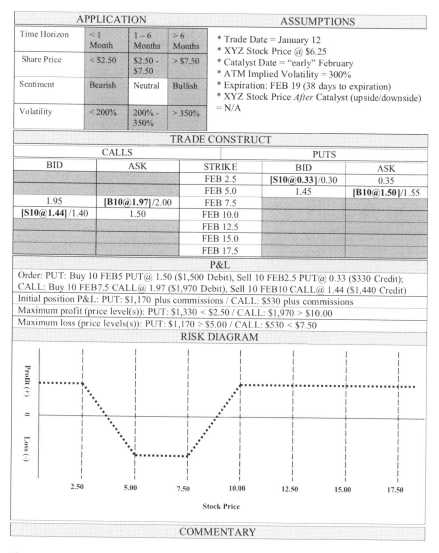

APPLICATION				ASSUMPTIONS
Time Horizon	< 1 Month	1 – 6 Months	> 6 Months	* Trade Date = January 12
Share Price	< $2.50	$2.50 - $7.50	> $7.50	* XYZ Stock Price @ $6.25
Sentiment	Bearish	Neutral	Bullish	* Catalyst Date = "early" February
Volatility	< 200%	200% - 350%	> 350%	* ATM Implied Volatility = 300%

* Expiration: FEB 19 (38 days to expiration)
* XYZ Stock Price *After* Catalyst (upside/downside) = N/A

TRADE CONSTRUCT

CALLS			PUTS	
BID	ASK	STRIKE	BID	ASK
		FEB 2.5	[S10@0.33]/0.30	0.35
		FEB 5.0	1.45	[B10@1.50]/1.55
1.95	[B10@1.97]/2.00	FEB 7.5		
[S10@1.44]/1.40	1.50	FEB 10.0		
		FEB 12.5		
		FEB 15.0		
		FEB 17.5		

P&L

Order: PUT: Buy 10 FEB5 PUT@ 1.50 ($1,500 Debit), Sell 10 FEB2.5 PUT@ 0.33 ($330 Credit);
CALL: Buy 10 FEB7.5 CALL@ 1.97 ($1,970 Debit), Sell 10 FEB10 CALL@ 1.44 ($1,440 Credit)
Initial position P&L: PUT: $1,170 plus commissions / CALL: $530 plus commissions
Maximum profit (price level(s)): PUT: $1,330 < $2.50 / CALL: $1,970 > $10.00
Maximum loss (price levels(s)): PUT: $1,170 > $5.00 / CALL: $530 < $7.50

RISK DIAGRAM

COMMENTARY

If you are able to trade ahead of the "crowd" by establishing a position well-in advance of a catalyst, a Put or Call buying strategy on a standalone basis can be quite powerful – you are basically buying options at discounted prices due to the lower level of implied volatility. Once the catalyst is near and implied volatility is high, however, you are buying expensive options – at this point in time, this is a strategy fraught with risk. Buying Puts or Calls as a standalone strategy is thus often a losing approach within the context of a near term FDA or clinical trial catalyst. A good alternative is to use the spread structure. A long Call spread involves buying a Call and selling a higher strike Call against it. Likewise, a long Put spread involves buying a Put and selling a lower strike Put against it. The long spread structure seeks to offset the high implied volatility you are buying with the high implied volatility you are selling – thus, in a way, canceling out the impact of high implied volatility at the initiation of the trade. In the example trade, XYZ is trading at $6.25 with a major catalyst approaching within a few weeks. Implied volatility is already at extremely high levels. A Call spread is initiated by buying 10 FEB 7.5 strike Call at 1.97 and selling 10 FEB 10.0 strike Call for 1.44. This trade costs $530 which is your risk in the trade. Maximum loss of $530 occurs if XYZ fails to settle above $7.50 by expiration. The breakeven price for the trade is approximately $8. Your maximum profit is $1,970 and is achieved when (if) XYZ settles above $10 by expiration. Likewise (and an entirely different trade), a long Put spread is initiated by buying 10 FEB 5.0 strike Put at 1.50 and selling 10 FEB 2.5 strike Put for 0.33. This trade costs $1,170 which, again, is your total risk in the trade. Maximum loss of $1,170 occurs if XYZ fails to settle below $5.00 by expiration. The breakeven price for the trade is approximately $3.80. Your maximum profit is $1,330 and is achieved when (if) XYZ settles below $2.50 by expiration. Trading spreads is the perfect risk / reward structure as total (potential) risk and total (potential) reward are defined precisely at the initiation of the trade (whereas in some structures total risk is defined but total reward is not and vice versa). In the Call example trade, our total risk is $530 and our total reward is $1,970. This fact permits the trader to make smarter trade decisions (where one assumes equal probabilities for various outcomes). For example and assuming equal probabilities, does it make more sense to do the

Call spread trade outlined in the example (risking $530 to make $1,970) or the Put spread trade (risking $1,170 to make $1,330)? This structure highlights these trade situations and allows for better decision-making or at the very least recognition of the risk you are taking to generated said reward.

6.3.4 Low Cost / No Cost Butterfly

APPLICATION				ASSUMPTIONS
Time Horizon	< 1 Month	1 – 6 Months	> 6 Months	* Trade Date(s) = December 1 – December 15
Share Price	< $2.50	$2.50 - $7.50	> $7.50	* XYZ Stock Price @ $9.00 - $11.00
Sentiment	Bearish	Neutral	Bullish	* Catalyst Date = December 15
Volatility	< 200%	200% - 350%	> 350%	* ATM Implied Volatility = 350%

Assumptions block:
* Trade Date(s) = December 1 – December 15
* XYZ Stock Price @ $9.00 - $11.00
* Catalyst Date = December 15
* ATM Implied Volatility = 350%
* Expiration: DEC 18 (17 days to expiration)
* XYZ Stock Price *After* Catalyst (upside/downside) = N/A

TRADE CONSTRUCT

CALLS		STRIKE	PUTS	
BID	ASK		BID	ASK
		DEC 2.5	.05	[B100@0.10]/0.15
		DEC 5.0	[S200@0.65]/0.60	0.70
		DEC 7.5	1.20	[B100@1.30]/1.35
		DEC 10.0		
1.60	[B100@1.75]/1.8	DEC 12.5		
[S200@1.40]/1.35	1.45	DEC 15.0		
0.85	[B100@0.95]/1.05	DEC 17.5		

P&L

Order: Buy 100 DEC2.5 PUT@ 0.10 ($1,000 Debit), Buy 100 DEC7.5 PUT@ 1.30 ($13,000 Debit), Buy 100 DEC12.5 CALL@ 1.75 ($17,500 Debit), Buy 100 DEC17.5 CALL@ 0.95 ($9,500 Debit), Sell 200 DEC5.0 PUT@ 0.65 ($13,000 Credit), Sell 200 DEC15.0 CALL@ 1.40 ($28,000 Credit)

Initial position P&L: $0 plus commissions

Maximum profit (price level(s)): $25,000 (@$5.00) PUT-side / $25,000 (@$15.00) CALL-side

Maximum loss (price levels(s)): $0 (< $2.50 > $7.50) PUT-side/ $0 (< $12.50 > $17.50) CALL-side

RISK DIAGRAM

Stock Price

COMMENTARY

This trade structure was discussed earlier in the book (please refer to Section 5.4, "Legging" In).   Basically, it involves establishing one or two (or more) butterflies (either long Put butterfly or long Call butterfly or both). This trade is best executed in the final month prior to a catalyst event. This trade requires a high level of intra-day volatility in addition to a high level of risk tolerance. The key to this strategy is strong planning and good execution. I recommend using a spreadsheet to track your trade-in values (if you are first unable to fill the entire order with your broker without the need to leg in). For example, Exhibit 6.3 demonstrates the building of a 50 X 100 X 50 butterfly position (not related to the trade example above). The position consisted of several trades at various strikes and various premium values. The spreadsheet allows you to track, in real-time, what your overall trade-in value is and allows you to continuously manage your position to achieve (hopefully) the desired overall trade-in value (which for this structure is a credit position). In the position below, the trade-in value was (0.03) per leg, a credit (i.e. a free trade).

Exhibit 6.3: Spreadsheet Position Tracker for Butterfly

5.0 Strike			7.5 Strike			10.0 Strike		
Contracts	Premium	Value	Contracts	Premium	Value	Contracts	Premium	Value
10	1.50	$1,500	-10	0.75	-$750	10	0.25	$250
10	1.25	$1,250	-10	1.00	-$1,000	15	0.30	$450
5	1.10	$550	-20	0.80	-$1,600	5	0.35	$175
15	1.30	$1,950	-40	0.95	-$3,800	5	0.35	$175
10	1.50	$1,500	-20	0.65	-$1,300	15	0.35	$525
50		$6,750	-100		-$8,450	50		$1,575
Butterfly Value								-$125
Premium value per leg (1 X 2 X 1)								-$0.03

As discussed earlier in the book, I would suggest building the position by initiating a series of long and short spread positions (that is, by starting with an equal contract long spread and finishing off with an equal contract short spread, resulting in a butterfly position). Using the strikes above as an example, that would be by buying 10 5.0 strike Call and Selling 10 7.5 strike Call followed by (i.e. after being filled) selling 10 more 7.5 strike Call and buying 10 10.0 strike Call. This technique limits your overall execution risk however it makes it much harder to achieve a credit position. If the approximate catalyst date is known and you have a higher risk tolerance (and there is a high level of intra-day volatility), you can leg in without using spreads as was done in Exhibit 6.3.

This may allow you to achieve a credit position easier but also exposes you to higher potential losses if there is an unexpected and unfavorable price spike or drop. If the catalyst date is imminent and unknown, as mentioned previously, I would highly suggest not initiating your leg-ins on the short side.

6.3.5 "One-Winged" Butterfly

APPLICATION				ASSUMPTIONS
Time Horizon	< 1 Month	1 – 6 Months	> 6 Months	* Trade Date = December 1
Share Price	< $2.50	$2.50 - $7.50	> $7.50	* XYZ Stock price @ $10.00 * Catalyst Date = December 15
Sentiment	Bearish	Neutral	Bullish	* ATM Implied Volatility = 300 ~ 500% * Expiration: DEC 18 (17 days to expiration)
Volatility	< 200%	200% - 350%	> 350%	* XYZ Stock Price *After* Catalyst (upside/downside) = N/A

TRADE CONSTRUCT					
CALLS			PUTS		
BID	ASK	STRIKE	BID		ASK
		DEC 2.5	[S200@0.10]/0.05		0.15
		DEC 5.0	0.25		[B100@0.30]/0.35
		DEC 7.5			
		DEC 10.0			
		DEC 12.5			
		DEC 15.0			
		DEC 17.5			

P&L
Order: Buy 100 DEC5.0 PUT @0.30 ($3,000 Debit), Sell 200 DEC2.5 PUT @0.10 ($2,000 Credit)
Initial position P&L: $1,000 Debit plus commissions
Maximum profit (price level(s)): $24,000((@$2.50)
Maximum loss (price levels(s)): $1,000 (>$5.00)

RISK DIAGRAM

COMMENTARY

A one-winged butterfly is basically a 0.0 / 2.5 / 5.0 strike Put butterfly. For example, one would sell two 2.5 strike Put for every one purchased 5.0 strike Put (the "zero" strike Put is free given that there are no zero strike Put as the stock cannot drop below zero). Because the "zero" strike Put is free, the economics of the trade structure can be quite favorable as the cash outlay is minimized (versus a full butterfly which requires the purchase of both "wings"). This structure works best when there is a month or less left prior to the catalyst event (even 1 day prior!), volatility is greater than 350% and the stock price is currently trading at prices greater than $7. One factor which optimizes the structure profit potential, for example, is a company with a single Phase III candidate, limited cash, and/or limited future alternatives should there be a failure. In such a situation, the stock should drop substantially and fall within the lower end of your profit zone, or approximately $0.00 to $2.50. If the company reports positive data, your initial position P&L will immediately be wiped out – you should not assume you can minimize your losses by trading out of the position as the 2.5 strike Put and 5.0 strike Put will immediately trade to 0.00 Bid / 0.05 Ask. If the catalyst event is negative for the stock and the stock drops significantly, you should seek to trade out of the position that same day as liquidity is maximized and implied volatility is still elevated. As mentioned with other structures, it is normally a bad idea to wait too long after the stock has made its move in these situations to close out your position. You will likely give back a lot of your profits as implied volatility will continue to drop and liquidity will quickly dry up (thus spreads, and your cost to trade, will increase).

6.3.6 "One-Winged" Butterfly – Time Variant

APPLICATION				ASSUMPTIONS

	APPLICATION			
Time Horizon	< 1 Month	1 – 6 Months	> 6 Months	
Share Price	< $2.50	$2.50 - $7.50	> $7.50	
Sentiment	Bearish	Neutral	Bullish	
Volatility	< 200%	200% - 350%	> 350%	

ASSUMPTIONS

* Trade Date = December 1
* XYZ Stock price @ $10.00
* Catalyst Date = **"mid-December"/unknown**
* ATM Implied Volatility = 350 ~ 500%
* Expiration: DEC 18 (17 days to expiration)
* XYZ Stock Price *After* Catalyst (upside/downside)
  = >$5.00/$1.50

TRADE CONSTRUCT

CALLS		STRIKE	PUTS	
BID	ASK		BID	ASK
		DEC 2.5		
		DEC 5.0	0.35	[B100@0.40]/0.45
		DEC 7.5		
		JAN 2.5	[S200@0.40]/0.35	0.45
		JAN 5.0		
		JAN 7.5		

P&L

Order: Buy 100 DEC5.0 PUT @0.40 ($4,000 Debit), Sell 200 JAN2.5 PUT @0.40 ($8,000 Credit)

Initial position P&L: $4,000 Credit plus commissions

Maximum profit (price level(s)): $29,000 (@$2.50) *Catalyst event **before** DEC options expiration*

Maximum loss (price levels(s)): +$4,000 (>$5.00) *Catalyst event **before** DEC options expiration*

Maximum profit (price level(s)): $4,000 (>$2.50) *Catalyst event **after** DEC options expiration*

Maximum loss (price levels(s)): $16,000 (@$1.50) *Catalyst event **after** DEC options expiration*

RISK DIAGRAM

COMMENTARY

This is one of my favorite trade structures because risk is defined by only one element: the timing of the announcement – nothing else matters (at least initially). In the example above, the "announcement" is to come in "December"

126

based on the company's press release. December (like all months) has four weeks and December options, like all options, expire in the third week. Thus the odds favor an announcement in the first three weeks. Due to the uncertainty, however, both December and January options are trading at very high levels of implied volatility (the 4th week of December is in the January option expiration). This permits the trade structure to function. A company will usually issue a press release stating the time for a conference call to discuss the results regarding the drug candidate. This usually comes on a Sunday night for an announcement on the following Monday morning although this is not a hard and fast rule. Assuming this falls before expiration of the December options, in this example, this structure will *immediately* result in a profit (for both positive and negative outcomes) given that the original trade produced a credit. If the results are negative, maximum profits may result. As mentioned, the key element in this trade is the time of the announcement. If you reach the Wednesday or Thursday preceding the Friday of the third week in the month, you need to make a decision. You have two choices: (a) close out the position (i.e. sell the long DEC 5.0 Put and buy back the JAN 2.5 Put) or (b) hold into the next week (i.e. let the DEC 5.0 Put expire and hold the JAN 2.5 short Put into results). Wednesday or Thursday (in the third week) is a good day to close out the position because the DEC 5.0 strike Put, in this example, will still have (some) value – you may thus minimize losses on this leg (remember, these options will expire worthless on Saturday and your last day to trade out will be Friday, where, lacking an announcement in the morning, will quickly become valueless – hence you will need to trade out on Wednesday or Thursday assuming you don't want to hold the 2.5 strike JAN Put into the next week). The JAN 2.5 Put will retain much of the value (or possibly increase in value) and as such, if you close out the position, expect a loss to equal the decline in value of the DEC 5.0 Put plus the spread paid to execute both sides of the trade (i.e. both the DEC 5.0 Put and DEC 2.5 Put) plus any gains on the short JAN 2.5 Put. If you allow the

DEC 5.0 strike Put to expire, your risk is defined on the short JAN 2.5 Put, and this risk can be quite substantial if results are *overly* negative (losses begin to accrue a few clicks below the 2.5 strike Put depending on the size of the credit generated in the initial trade).

An important note regarding this structure: it is essential to be aware of the risks and to trade with an iron-clad plan. If you are overly risk averse or unable to force a loss to avoid larger potential future losses, this trade structure should be avoided.

6.3.7 "Short Strike" Iron Butterfly

APPLICATION				ASSUMPTIONS
Time Horizon	< 1 Month	1 – 6 Months	> 6 Months	* Trade Date = December 1 * XYZ Stock Price @ $1.10
Share Price	< $2.50	$2.50 - $7.50	> $7.50	* Catalyst Date = December 15 * ATM Implied Volatility = 450%+
Sentiment	Bearish	Neutral	Bullish	* Expiration: DEC 18 (17 days to expiration) * XYZ Stock Price *After* Catalyst (upside/downside) = N/A
Volatility	< 200%	200% - 350%	> 350%	

TRADE CONSTRUCT				
CALLS			PUTS	
BID	ASK	STRIKE	BID	ASK
		DEC 1.0	0.40	**[B200@0.44]** /0.45
[S200@0.15] /0.15	0.20	DEC 1.5	**[S200@0.82]** /0.80	0.85
0.05	**[B200@0.08]** /0.10	DEC 2.0		
		DEC 2.5		
		DEC 3.0		
		DEC 5.0		
		DEC 7.5		

P&L
Order: Sell 200 DEC1.5 CALL@ 0.15 ($3,000 Credit), Sell 200 DEC1.5 PUT@ 0.82 ($16,400 Credit), Buy 200 DEC2.0 CALL@ 0.08 ($1,600 Debit), Buy 200 DEC1.0 PUT@ 0.44 ($8,800 Debit)
Initial position P&L: +$9,000 plus commissions
Maximum profit (price level(s)): $9,000 between $1 and $2
Maximum loss (price levels(s)): $1,000 loss incurs < $1.05 and > $1.95

RISK DIAGRAM

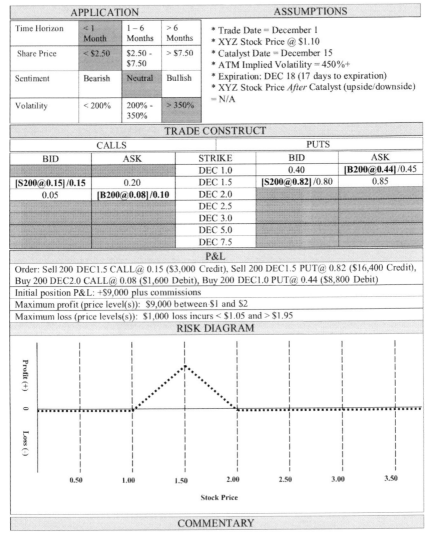

COMMENTARY

This structure is best suited for situations where option strike prices are spaced in 0.50 to 1.00 increments (as opposed to 2.5 to 5.0 increments), where implied volatility is greater than 450% and where there is a **very** high level of volume both in the options and the underlying stock. These types of situations are often characterized by a high level of day-trader activity, unsubstantiated rumors, bear raids, price spikes, etc. This high level of volatility allows a nimble and patient trader to establish unusually low risk / high reward trades. It should be possible to initiate *in-the-money* trades (i.e. within the confines of the Iron Butterfly, or in context of the example trade above, between the 1.0 and 2.0 strikes) where one risks $1 with the potential to generate $10 – highly unusual indeed. This structure functions best when the catalyst event date is unknown yet apparently imminent. Initiate the trade **early in the second week of the expiration month**. This will allow you to capture the "pumped up" premium values. In the trade example above, we sell 200 1.5 strike Call and Put and buy 200 1.0 strike Put and 200 2.0 strike Call for a credit of $9,000. Our total risk in the trade is $1,000 – thus this represents a 9 to 1 return for an in-the-money trade. The primary goal of the Short Strike Iron Butterfly trade structure is to have the catalyst announcement date occur *after* the options expire while maintaining the share price within the confines of the Iron Butterfly, preferably close to $1.50. As expiration approaches, the position will normally show a profit (unless the share price has dropped or risen beyond the confines of the Iron Butterfly; in some cases, it may show a profit no matter where it trades). If you show a profit prior to expiration, consider closing out the position. The high level of liquidity should permit an exit without too much slippage.

6.3.8 Time Spread (Position Build)

<table>
<tr><td colspan="4">APPLICATION</td><td colspan="2">ASSUMPTIONS</td></tr>
<tr>
<td>Time Horizon</td>
<td>< 1 Month</td>
<td>1 – 6 Months</td>
<td>> 6 Months</td>
<td colspan="2" rowspan="5">
* Trade Date = May 1
* XYZ Stock price @ $4 (Jun) / $5 (Aug) / $6 (Oct) / $7 (Dec)
* Catalyst Date = December 15
* ATM Implied Volatility = 150%
* Expiration: DEC 18 (228 days to expiration)
* XYZ Stock Price *After* Catalyst (upside/downside) => $10.00/< $7.50
</td>
</tr>
<tr>
<td>Share Price</td>
<td>< $2.50</td>
<td>$2.50 - $7.50</td>
<td>> $7.50</td>
</tr>
<tr>
<td>Sentiment</td>
<td>Bearish</td>
<td>Neutral</td>
<td>Bullish</td>
</tr>
<tr>
<td>Volatility</td>
<td>< 200%</td>
<td>200% - 350%</td>
<td>> 350%</td>
</tr>
</table>

TRADE CONSTRUCT

CALLS			PUTS	
BID	ASK	STRIKE	BID	ASK
[S10@0.20]/ 0.15	0.25	JUN 7.5(a)	Stock price= $4	
[S10@0.55]/ 0.50	0.60	AUG 7.5(b)	Stock price= $5	
[S10@0.95]/ 0.90	1.00	OCT 7.5(c)	Stock price= $6	
1.00	[B10@1.10]/1.20	DEC 7.5(a)	Stock price= $4	
[S10@0.85]/ 0.80	0.90	DEC 10.0(d)	Stock price= $7	

P&L

Order: (a) Buy 10 DEC7.5 CALL @1.10 ($1,100 Debit), Sell 10 JUN7.5 CALL @0.20 ($200 Credit) (b) Sell 10 AUG7.5 CALL @0.55 ($550 Credit) (c) Sell 10 OCT7.5 CALL @0.95 ($950 Credit) (d) Sell 10 DEC10 CALL @0.85 ($850 Credit)
Initial position P&L: $900 Debit plus commissions
Maximum profit (price level(s)): $3,950 (>$10.00)
Maximum loss (price levels(s)): +$1,450 (<$7.50) * assuming price increases but not > $7.50
Maximum theoretical loss: $900 * assuming stock declines and there is no interim 7.5 premium to sell

RISK DIAGRAM

COMMENTARY

The (long) Call time spread is a fairly basic position: buy a far expiration Call option and sell a nearer term expiration Call option at the same strike. This structure can be quite powerful when applied to small cap biotech catalyst events. Normally, over a period of six to nine months prior to a catalyst event, the small cap biotech stock price will increase as the market begins to "price in" a potential upside move. The stock price will also (brilliantly) tend to approach prior technical levels (where relevant). Further benefiting this structure is the gradual increase in volatility which thus results in higher successive premium which can be sold against the longer term option. These elements in aggregate often create the perfect situation for this structure. In the example above the catalyst event is around eight to nine months away. The strike to focus on is determined by prior technical levels or simply availability and/or liquidity of strikes. In the example we are able to sell 7.5 Call strike premium in three successive option expirations (JUN, AUG, OCT) against the purchased DEC 7.5 Call (the month of the catalyst event). After the OCT 7.5 Call expires, you have an option to sell the higher strike (DEC 10.0 Call strike) which caps your upside but provides a decent return on the overall trade if there is a failed result. The biggest risk of the structure occurs during the first two expirations (if the stock rockets up and past the DEC 7.5 Call or if there is some news disaster, such as a death in one of the trials, which would send the shares plummeting. The (initial) primary objective of the structure is to build a position and to achieve, in effect, a "free" trade (or even better, a credit position); that is, where the premium sold exceeds the initial cost of the longer term option. In the final month of the trade you either can hold the 7.5 Call into expiration or, if you are more risk averse, and as mentioned, sell the DEC 10.0 Call to create a bull Call spread, which will provide a decent profit for the trade even with a failed event.

6.3.9 Hedged Time Spread

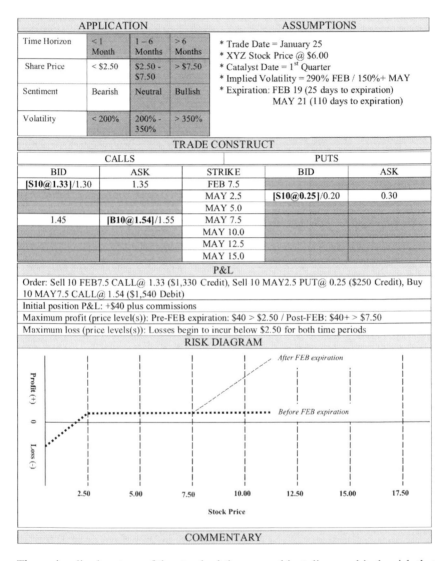

APPLICATION				ASSUMPTIONS
Time Horizon	< 1 Month	1 – 6 Months	> 6 Months	* Trade Date = January 25
Share Price	< $2.50	$2.50 - $7.50	> $7.50	* XYZ Stock Price @ $6.00 * Catalyst Date = 1st Quarter * Implied Volatility = 290% FEB / 150%+ MAY
Sentiment	Bearish	Neutral	Bullish	* Expiration: FEB 19 (25 days to expiration) MAY 21 (110 days to expiration)
Volatility	< 200%	200% - 350%	> 350%	

TRADE CONSTRUCT				
CALLS			PUTS	
BID	ASK	STRIKE	BID	ASK
[S10@1.33]/1.30	1.35	FEB 7.5		
		MAY 2.5	[S10@0.25]/0.20	0.30
		MAY 5.0		
1.45	[B10@1.54]/1.55	MAY 7.5		
		MAY 10.0		
		MAY 12.5		
		MAY 15.0		

P&L
Order: Sell 10 FEB7.5 CALL@ 1.33 ($1,330 Credit), Sell 10 MAY2.5 PUT@ 0.25 ($250 Credit), Buy 10 MAY7.5 CALL@ 1.54 ($1,540 Debit)
Initial position P&L: +$40 plus commissions
Maximum profit (price level(s)): Pre-FEB expiration: $40 > $2.50 / Post-FEB: $40+ > $7.50
Maximum loss (price levels(s)): Losses begin to incur below $2.50 for both time periods

RISK DIAGRAM

After FEB expiration

Before FEB expiration

Profit (+)   0   Loss (-)

2.50   5.00   7.50   10.00   12.50   15.00   17.50

Stock Price

COMMENTARY

The major disadvantage of the standard time spread just discussed is the risk that the stock will move beyond the sold strike prior to said strike's expiration – this can be somewhat frustrating, especially for positions held a long time and near to the front month expiration. For example, I once had a JAN/MAY 5.0 strike

Call time spread. ***Four days*** prior to the expiration of the JAN 5.0 strike Call, major news was announced and the spread collapsed (the stock rocketed up $2 a share). I not only lost the accrued P&L but also the initial debit cost of the position (if the front month had expired, I would have made substantial profits). In order to avoid this issue consider using what I call a Hedged Time Spread. In this position, you are basically getting paid to use the structure. This is possible because you are selling a Put as a part of the trade (and of course taking additional risk). Assume stock XYZ is currently trading at $6.00 in late January. The company is slated to announce major clinical trial results in the "1st quarter." Since you are in late January, there are only two remaining expiration series left in the 1st quarter: FEB and MAR. Under a normal time spread structure, you would take advantage of the higher implied volatility by selling either the FEB or MAR series against a further, significantly lower implied volatility expiration month, such as MAY. Since the news could come at any time, the right series to choose to sell, under this structure, would be the FEB (the earliest to expire). Based on the example in the table above, you would sell 10 FEB 7.50 strike Call for 1.33 against 10 MAY 7.5 strike Call for 1.54. The trade nets to a $210 debit. As mentioned, if positive news comes out prior to the FEB expiration, you risk losing the entire debit (in this example, $210). To hedge this risk, sell the MAY 2.5 strike Put for 0.25. This is now a credit position – i.e. you are being paid to use this structure (albeit not very much in this example). If the news comes out prior to FEB expiration, and the stock jumps and settles above the 7.5 Call strike, you profit by the amount of the credit (of course you have to wait until the Put expires). If the news does not come out or if the stock fails to settle above the 7.50 Call strike on the news, you are now in a near free trade position (after the expiration of the FEB 7.5 Calls). In this situation, you can decide to exit, hold or take some additional operation such as selling the MAY 10.0 strike Calls (thus further enhancing the profitability of the position). It is important to note that the credit position generated by the structure comes with added risk: a significant drop in the shares will incur a loss (often substantial) if the shares trade below the Put strike. Given this risk, the Hedged Time Spread structure should only be used when the company is financially solid and/or has other near to medium term catalysts (as you may end up being assigned the shares under a negative scenario) – in such a situation, this can be a powerful structure.

6.3.10 Long Term Put Sale

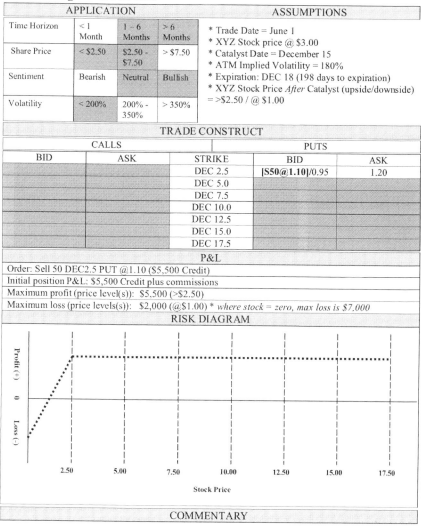

APPLICATION				ASSUMPTIONS
Time Horizon	< 1 Month	1 - 6 Months	> 6 Months	* Trade Date = June 1
Share Price	< $2.50	$2.50 - $7.50	> $7.50	* XYZ Stock price @ $3.00
Sentiment	Bearish	Neutral	Bullish	* Catalyst Date = December 15
Volatility	< 200%	200% - 350%	> 350%	* ATM Implied Volatility = 180%

Assumptions:
* Trade Date = June 1
* XYZ Stock price @ $3.00
* Catalyst Date = December 15
* ATM Implied Volatility = 180%
* Expiration: DEC 18 (198 days to expiration)
* XYZ Stock Price *After* Catalyst (upside/downside) = >$2.50 / @ $1.00

TRADE CONSTRUCT

CALLS		STRIKE	PUTS	
BID	ASK		BID	ASK
		DEC 2.5	[S50@1.10]/0.95	1.20
		DEC 5.0		
		DEC 7.5		
		DEC 10.0		
		DEC 12.5		
		DEC 15.0		
		DEC 17.5		

P&L

Order: Sell 50 DEC2.5 PUT @1.10 ($5,500 Credit)

Initial position P&L: $5,500 Credit plus commissions

Maximum profit (price level(s)): $5,500 (>$2.50)

Maximum loss (price levels(s)): $2,000 (@$1.00) * *where stock = zero, max loss is $7,000*

RISK DIAGRAM

COMMENTARY

The long term Put sale benefits from some of the same elements supporting the Time spread already discussed: small cap biotech stock prices tend to increase over the six to nine months preceding a FDA or clinical trial catalyst event. The increase in the share price, in most cases, tends to outpace the increase in implied volatility (which hurts the position P&L). This is a longer term, strategic trade and thus requires a higher level of due diligence given that you could end up owning the shares if the stock declines and you are assigned the shares (assuming you don't close out the position). Further complicating the trade is the (usual) lack of liquidity which may appear to "trap" you in the trade given a volatile and changing/widening Bid / Ask spread and thus a high price to pay if you want to try and exit. This trade is best suited for companies with strong fundamentals, such as a more diverse or deeper drug development pipeline, solid cash balances and a transparent source of future cash. The key point is to only do this trade for the strongest companies that you will feel comfortable owning the shares despite the high level of volatility. In this trade, your goal should be to sell the Put where the premium minus the share price overlaps with the company's cash per share value (where possible) or at least comes close. For example, in the example above, XYZ stock trades at $3.00. The company has cash on the balance sheet of 100 million and 50 million shares outstanding, which equates to $2.00 per share (= $100mln / 50mln). It is possible to sell the DEC 2.5 Put at 1.10. The share price minus the premium equates to $1.90 (= $3.00 - $1.10). In this example, our trade-in price overlaps by $0.10 with cash value per share which means that our trade duration risk is now below a dirty "liquidation value" discussed early in this book – this is a good trade. Trades like this do not only exist in theory (or in books such as this) – they are out there and you simply need to do some work to find them. One final comment about liquidity and this trade structure. As mentioned above, you will likely, in popular vernacular, be married to the position once you trade into it. While you hold the position be prepared to encounter volatile, often bizarre, movements in the Bid / Ask spread. As such, depending on the size of the position, you will have large, often meaningless, swings in P&L from time to time. Do not concern yourself (and do not panic!) with these swings as most will self-correct over time.

6.3.11 Extreme Volatility Covered Call

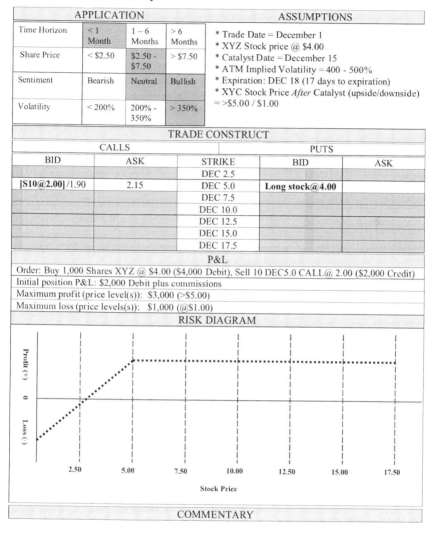

APPLICATION				ASSUMPTIONS

	< 1 Month	1 – 6 Months	> 6 Months	
Time Horizon	< 1 Month	1 – 6 Months	> 6 Months	* Trade Date = December 1
Share Price	< $2.50	$2.50 - $7.50	> $7.50	* XYZ Stock price @ $4.00
Sentiment	Bearish	Neutral	Bullish	* Catalyst Date = December 15
Volatility	< 200%	200% - 350%	> 350%	* ATM Implied Volatility = 400 - 500%

Assumptions:
* Trade Date = December 1
* XYZ Stock price @ $4.00
* Catalyst Date = December 15
* ATM Implied Volatility = 400 - 500%
* Expiration: DEC 18 (17 days to expiration)
* XYC Stock Price *After* Catalyst (upside/downside)
= >$5.00 / $1.00

TRADE CONSTRUCT

CALLS			PUTS	
BID	ASK	STRIKE	BID	ASK
		DEC 2.5		
[S10@2.00]/1.90	2.15	DEC 5.0	Long stock@4.00	
		DEC 7.5		
		DEC 10.0		
		DEC 12.5		
		DEC 15.0		
		DEC 17.5		

P&L

Order: Buy 1,000 Shares XYZ @ $4.00 ($4,000 Debit), Sell 10 DEC5.0 CALL@ 2.00 ($2,000 Credit)
Initial position P&L: $2,000 Debit plus commissions
Maximum profit (price level(s)): $3,000 (>$5.00)
Maximum loss (price level(s)): $1,000 (@$1.00)

RISK DIAGRAM

COMMENTARY

The extreme volatility covered Call is a basic strategy with potential for outsized returns. As you are likely aware, it involves buying or owning the shares and selling an equivalent amount of at-the-money or further out-of-the-money Call options against the share position. It is not uncommon to generate returns of greater than 30% with some downside protection. A key factor in this structure is to determine how much the shares will drop with negative results – this is the key risk. It is very important to stress the following: **for nearly all negative outcome situations, the Call premium sold will be insufficient to offset losses on the shares.** As such, if this structure is used, it is absolutely essential to make sure you understand the downside risk. Aside from analyst estimates, a good market based method as discussed earlier in this book, is to use the at-the-money straddle to estimate the potential downside. For example, if the shares are trading at $10, and the at-the-money straddle (i.e. the 10.0 strike) is trading at $4, the market is estimating a move of potentially down to $6. If you sold the 10.0 strike Call for $2.5, this would give you downside protection to $7.50. If the shares moved to the price implied by the at-the-money straddle, you would lose an additional $1.5 on the downside. This is actually not bad, since you are "risking" $1.5 to make $2.5. However, what is implied is not always what happens – in small cap biotech, extreme movements, beyond expectations, are usually the norm. As such, and depending on your risk tolerance, it is probably good to assume an even more extreme downward move. If the shares dropped to $1, for example, the position would show massive losses. Therefore it is important for you to determine how much risk you are willing to take prior to using this structure. On a final note, this structure works great as a trade going into a run-up. In such situations, once (and if) the shares run-up prior to a catalyst, the position can be closed out and the profits can be rolled into another structure more suitable for the immediate catalyst event.

6.3.12 Short Straddle

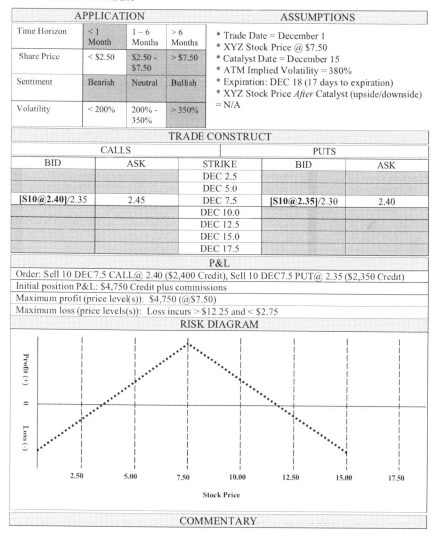

APPLICATION				ASSUMPTIONS	
Time Horizon	< 1 Month	1 – 6 Months	> 6 Months	* Trade Date = December 1	
Share Price	< $2.50	$2.50 - $7.50	> $7.50	* XYZ Stock Price @ $7.50 * Catalyst Date = December 15	
Sentiment	Bearish	Neutral	Bullish	* ATM Implied Volatility = 380% * Expiration: DEC 18 (17 days to expiration)	
Volatility	< 200%	200% - 350%	> 350%	* XYZ Stock Price *After* Catalyst (upside/downside) = N/A	

TRADE CONSTRUCT					
CALLS			PUTS		
BID	ASK	STRIKE	BID	ASK	
		DEC 2.5			
		DEC 5.0			
[S10@2.40]/2.35	2.45	DEC 7.5	[S10@2.35]/2.30	2.40	
		DEC 10.0			
		DEC 12.5			
		DEC 15.0			
		DEC 17.5			

P&L
Order: Sell 10 DEC7.5 CALL@ 2.40 ($2,400 Credit), Sell 10 DEC7.5 PUT@ 2.35 ($2,350 Credit)
Initial position P&L: $4,750 Credit plus commissions
Maximum profit (price level(s)): $4,750 (@$7.50)
Maximum loss (price levels(s)): Loss incurs > $12.25 and < $2.75

RISK DIAGRAM

Profit (+) 0 Loss (-)

2.50   5.00   7.50   10.00   12.50   15.00   17.50

Stock Price

COMMENTARY

This trade structure is a pure play on the collapse in implied volatility following a catalyst event. As you are now aware, implied volatility going into a catalyst event is nearly always greater than 250% and often above 400%. Following an announcement, implied volatility will drop substantially (in the low triple/high double digits) thus generating gains on the sold Put and Call position irrespective of direction of price movement (at least to the break-even points). Most of the risk in this structure will be on an outsized upward move in the shares given that small cap biotech stock prices are usually below $5.00 thus giving "more room to move" on the upside. As such, it is important to understand the nature of the drug candidate and to determine potential upside movement. It is usually a good idea to avoid this structure for drug candidates that are deemed potential "blockbusters" as the share price increase may cause you to suffer significant losses (for example, this would have been a disastrous strategy if used for Dendreon's catalyst announcement). It is also important to monitor short interest (greater than 20%) in the shares that could also contribute to additional violent upward share movement. The addition of the short Put element adds an additional level of complexity to the position. As discussed in the trade structure review of selling Puts, you need to make sure you understand the financial robustness of the company (or lack thereof) and plan accordingly. This is usually best done prior to the catalyst event (i.e. the decision to close-out or be assigned the shares on a negative outcome). A good potential idea if you like the shares and there is a failed event is to be assigned the shares and then immediately sell Calls against them to recoup losses (if any). For example, stock XYZ trades at $5 and you sell a 5.0 strike straddle for $3 (sell equal amounts of 5.0 strike Call and 5.0 strike Put). The news is negative and XYZ drops to $2. You show no profit or loss (5 - 3 = 2 - 2 = 0). You allow the 5.0 strike Call to expire and are assigned the shares from the sold 5.0 strike Put. On the next expiration, you sell the 2.5 strike Call against your held shares for $0.50 and continue to repeat until you are taken out or decide to hold the shares. For upside scenarios, it is almost always a good idea to immediately (once Bid / Ask spreads compress) close out the position following the announcement (i.e. on the same day). As mentioned earlier in this book, this permits an exit at the height of liquidity.

6.3.13 Short Strangle

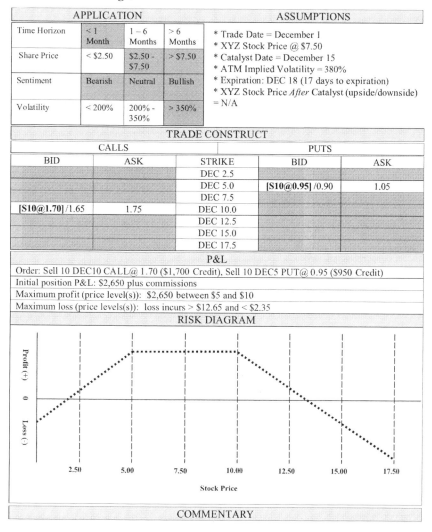

APPLICATION				ASSUMPTIONS
Time Horizon	< 1 Month	1 – 6 Months	> 6 Months	* Trade Date = December 1
Share Price	< $2.50	$2.50 - $7.50	> $7.50	* XYZ Stock Price @ $7.50 * Catalyst Date = December 15 * ATM Implied Volatility = 380%
Sentiment	Bearish	Neutral	Bullish	* Expiration: DEC 18 (17 days to expiration) * XYZ Stock Price *After* Catalyst (upside/downside)
Volatility	< 200%	200% - 350%	> 350%	= N/A

TRADE CONSTRUCT					
CALLS			PUTS		
BID	ASK	STRIKE	BID	ASK	
		DEC 2.5			
		DEC 5.0	[S10@0.95] /0.90	1.05	
		DEC 7.5			
[S10@1.70] /1.65	1.75	DEC 10.0			
		DEC 12.5			
		DEC 15.0			
		DEC 17.5			

P&L
Order: Sell 10 DEC10 CALL@ 1.70 ($1,700 Credit), Sell 10 DEC5 PUT@ 0.95 ($950 Credit)
Initial position P&L: $2,650 plus commissions
Maximum profit (price level(s)): $2,650 between $5 and $10
Maximum loss (price levels(s)): loss incurs > $12.65 and < $2.35

RISK DIAGRAM

COMMENTARY

The Short Strangle plays off of the same elements as the Short Straddle (collapse in implied volatility) however at wider strikes. In the example above, a Short Strangle is constructed around the XYZ share price of 7.5 by selling an equal amount of 5.0 strike Put and 10.0 strike Call. The same risk elements need to be assessed as with the Short Straddle (upside and downside risk). The wider strike range decreases the risk exposure however at the cost of additional premium. As such, many will sell more contracts to compensate for the loss of additional premium – avoid this route as it could lead to substantial losses if you are wrong. As with other structures of this type, decide in advance on the strategy for both a negative and positive outcome and if a decision to close out the position occurs, do it following the announcement on the same day.

6.3.14 "Split Month" Spread

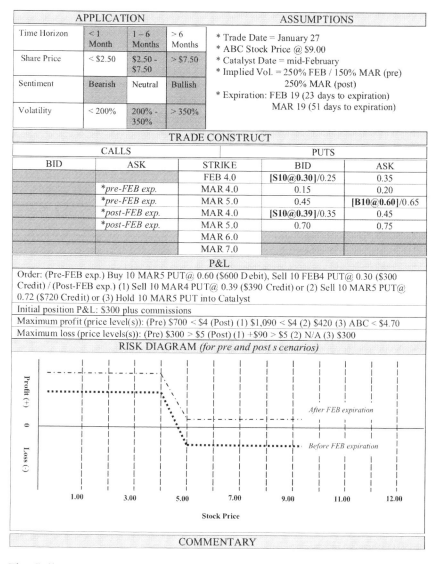

<table>
<tr><td colspan="4">APPLICATION</td><td colspan="3">ASSUMPTIONS</td></tr>
</table>

APPLICATION				ASSUMPTIONS
Time Horizon	< 1 Month	1 – 6 Months	> 6 Months	* Trade Date = January 27
Share Price	< $2.50	$2.50 - $7.50	> $7.50	* ABC Stock Price @ $9.00 * Catalyst Date = mid-February * Implied Vol. = 250% FEB / 150% MAR (pre)
Sentiment	Bearish	Neutral	Bullish	250% MAR (post) * Expiration: FEB 19 (23 days to expiration)
Volatility	< 200%	200% - 350%	> 350%	MAR 19 (51 days to expiration)

TRADE CONSTRUCT

CALLS			PUTS	
BID	ASK	STRIKE	BID	ASK
		FEB 4.0	[S10@0.30]/0.25	0.35
	*pre-FEB exp.	MAR 4.0	0.15	0.20
	*pre-FEB exp.	MAR 5.0	0.45	[B10@0.60]/0.65
	*post-FEB exp.	MAR 4.0	[S10@0.39]/0.35	0.45
	*post-FEB exp.	MAR 5.0	0.70	0.75
		MAR 6.0		
		MAR 7.0		

P&L

Order: (Pre-FEB exp.) Buy 10 MAR5 PUT@ 0.60 ($600 Debit), Sell 10 FEB4 PUT@ 0.30 ($300 Credit) / (Post-FEB exp.) (1) Sell 10 MAR4 PUT@ 0.39 ($390 Credit) or (2) Sell 10 MAR5 PUT@ 0.72 ($720 Credit) or (3) Hold 10 MAR5 PUT into Catalyst

Initial position P&L: $300 plus commissions

Maximum profit (price level(s)): (Pre) $700 < $4 (Post) (1) $1,090 < $4 (2) $420 (3) ABC < $4.70

Maximum loss (price levels(s)): (Pre) $300 > $5 (Post) (1) +$90 > $5 (2) N/A (3) $300

RISK DIAGRAM *(for pre and post scenarios)*

COMMENTARY

The Split Month Spread seeks to benefit from the attributes of a long spread structure while exploiting the (often substantial) differences in implied volatility between a catalyst month and a post-catalyst month. This structure is kind of a "turbo charged" long Call or long Put spread. This structure is best used when a FDA or clinical trial catalyst is expected in one month but the date is still uncertain (i.e. the news is expected in either early or mid-February, for example, but could come out after February expiration). Often in these situations, implied volatility is significantly higher in the expected month than the following month – this allows the structure to function. In the trade example, ABC is expected to receive news on whether or not their drug is approved in mid-February. The market is collectively thinking this news will come prior to FEB expiration as evidenced by the enormous discrepancy between implied volatility between FEB and MAR options. In the example, we structure a bearish trade by selling 10 FEB 4.0 strike Put for 0.30 and simultaneously buying 10 MAR 5.0 strike Put for 0.60. The net cost is a $300 debit that represents your maximum risk in the trade. It should be noted that this trade works best where there are $1 increment strikes (as opposed to $2.50 increments). One very good aspect of this structure is the large amount of optionality it provides you as a trader. First, if the news is negative and ABC stock drops past $4.00 by expiration, our maximum profit is $700 (if positive, our maximum loss is the original debit as mentioned of $300). Here is where the trade gets really interesting: if the news does not come out prior to FEB expiration, the sold FEB Puts expire worthless and you now maintain several new choices. First, implied volatility on the MAR series will immediately rocket higher (most likely matching the FEB implied volatility prior to expiration). In such a scenario, MAR implied volatility increase from 150% to 250% (where FEB 5.0 strike Put implied volatility was prior to expiration). In this situation, our MAR 5.0 strike Puts increase in value from 0.60 to 0.72 (this is on top of the proceeds from the expired sold FEB 4.0 strike Puts). At this juncture we can simply sell the Puts and take our profits without having to risk holding through the catalyst: nice situation. Another alternative would be to sell the MAR 4.0 strike Puts against our MAR 5.0 strike Puts. In this situation, we sell the MAR 4.0 strike Put for

0.39; in this example, we have basically reduced our risk from 0.30 per spread to a credit per spread of 0.09. If the news is negative and ABC stock drops below $4.00 by expiration, our maximum profit is $1,090. Since we now have a credit situation, if the news is positive and the stock jumps, our maximum loss is *a gain* of $90. Finally, and if we are feeling lucky, we can always leave the MAR 5.0 strike Put free and clear – under a negative scenario (for the shares), our maximum profit can be quite substantial. For example, if this is the company's only product candidate the stock could drop to cash per share value. Assuming ABC has cash per share of $1.50, and the shares drop to this value under the free and clear MAR 5.0 strike Put scenario, our profit is around $3,200.

6.3.15 "The Box"

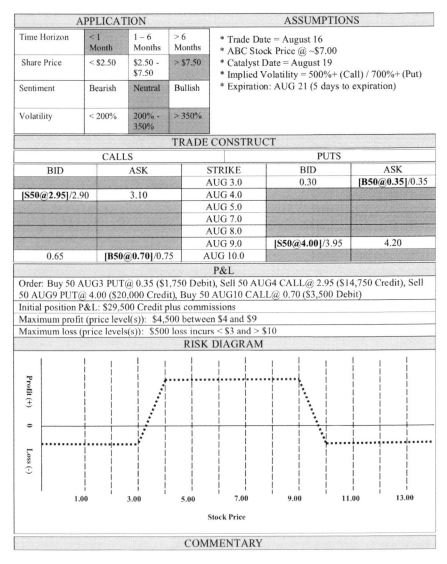

APPLICATION				ASSUMPTIONS	
Time Horizon	< 1 Month	1 – 6 Months	> 6 Months	* Trade Date = August 16	
Share Price	< $2.50	$2.50 - $7.50	> $7.50	* ABC Stock Price @ ~$7.00 * Catalyst Date = August 19	
Sentiment	Bearish	Neutral	Bullish	* Implied Volatility = 500%+ (Call) / 700%+ (Put) * Expiration: AUG 21 (5 days to expiration)	
Volatility	< 200%	200% - 350%	> 350%		

TRADE CONSTRUCT					
CALLS			PUTS		
BID	ASK	STRIKE	BID	ASK	
		AUG 3.0	0.30	[B50@0.35]/0.35	
[S50@2.95]/2.90	3.10	AUG 4.0			
		AUG 5.0			
		AUG 7.0			
		AUG 8.0			
		AUG 9.0	[S50@4.00]/3.95	4.20	
0.65	[B50@0.70]/0.75	AUG 10.0			

P&L

Order: Buy 50 AUG3 PUT@ 0.35 ($1,750 Debit), Sell 50 AUG4 CALL@ 2.95 ($14,750 Credit), Sell 50 AUG9 PUT@ 4.00 ($20,000 Credit), Buy 50 AUG10 CALL@ 0.70 ($3,500 Debit)

Initial position P&L: $29,500 Credit plus commissions

Maximum profit (price level(s)): $4,500 between $4 and $9

Maximum loss (price levels(s)): $500 loss incurs < $3 and > $10

RISK DIAGRAM

COMMENTARY

The Box (others give it a different name) is best applied to situations with extreme levels of implied volatility: i.e. north of 500%. This strategy is optimized where there is a significant difference between levels of implied

147

volatility between Puts and Calls (i.e. one is substantially higher than the other). This strategy can produce very favorable risk / reward set-ups and on (very) rare occasions, produce an arbitrage situation (i.e. risk free money). This strategy is best implemented a week or two prior to a major catalyst with a specific date (such as an Advisory Panel or PDUFA). Also, this structure is usually only possible where there are 1.0 strike increments (as opposed to 2.50 increments). In the example trade, an Advisory Panel for ABC's drug candidate is slated to take place on a Thursday in the third week in August (i.e. right before the AUG series expires). ABC is trading at $7.00 a share on Monday (before release of the briefing docs). Ideally this trade structure should be put in place prior to the release of the briefing docs in order to capture maximum implied volatility (although some discretion can be taken to fit the circumstances). This structure is a bit tricky as you need to test it at several different strikes equidistant from the mid-point, i.e. the current share price). In the trade example (after many iterations at different strikes) we determine that the optimal strike mix is the 3/4/9/10 strike set – this is the mix where the cost of the trade is the lowest. In the example trade, we buy 50 AUG 3.0 strike Puts at 0.35, sell 50 AUG 4.0 strike Call at 2.95, sell 50 AUG 9.0 strike Put at 4.00 and buy 50 AUG 10.0 strike Call at 0.70 for a total *credit* per set of 5.90 or a total of $29,500. The maximum risk in the trade is $500 (often, in very volatile markets, the maximum risk is actually a credit; i.e. **the most you can lose is to gain the credit** – an arbitrage situation; do not think this is a Wall Street myth, I have achieved this and so can you). Our maximum profit, in the example trade, is $4,500 and is achieved if ABC shares trade approximately between the inner bound strikes, in the example trade, $4 and $10. Several notes need to be made about execution and management of this structure. First, when (if) you get filled, expect a substantial negative P&L impact. This is the impact of the (often) wide spreads from all of the component strikes in the structure being priced at mid-value by your broker. Don't worry about this situation as the most you can lose if the structure stays intact is $500 (for the example). This usually corrects from several hours to a few days. Second, care needs to be taken with regards to early exercise of the sold Calls and Puts in the structure (in the example trade the 4.0 strike Call and the 9.0 strike Put) – make sure to check the Delta of each: if either is above 95 (or -95) there is a high risk of early exercise which means you get short shares (for the Calls) and long shares (for the Puts). This situation can be very unfavorable due to "hard to borrow" fees (most stocks facing these events are deemed "hard to borrow" given high levels of short interest) or, even worse, forced buy-ins for the short shares where your broker forces you to cover the short shares and charges you a penalty (also leaves your structure out of balance which could be quite dangerous should the shares be halted). In these situations, you can either (1) re-balance the structure (i.e. have equal contracts for each strike) by clearing out the shares (either short or long from exercised short Calls or Puts) while (immediately) filling the required strikes with new options (thus maintaining the same contract level) or (2) reduce the elements out of balance to put the structure back into balance although at a smaller level of total contracts.

The Box structure is extremely difficult to manage and should only be attempted by individuals with a high level of experience managing complex option positions and a high level of risk tolerance.

6.4   A FEW NOTES ABOUT PHASE I/II TRADES

During your analysis and search for opportunities, you may encounter tradable situations for companies with only early stage drug candidates in their pipeline (i.e. Phase I and Phase II). A select few trading strategies when applied to these companies/situations are discussed below.

6.4.1   Put Sale Pre–Announcement

For promising companies that you intend to build a long term share position, a good idea is to sell Put pre-Phase I/II announcement(s). In such cases, you benefit from the collapse in the high implied volatility options (you sold the premium) and can potentially pick up the shares, assuming you are assigned, at a lower cost basis. Again, when selling Puts, remember that a higher level of due diligence is required.

6.4.2   Short Shares Post–Positive Phase I/II Announcement

One highly effective strategy is to short the shares of a company immediately following a *positive* Phase I/II announcement. A successful announcement will ignite short covering (and some misguided and jubilant retail buying) and thus send the stock rocketing up. As the drug candidate has several more years of development and many potential pitfalls including the potential of total failure, the shares should invariably trade back down over the next several days. Assuming you can get "borrow" (i.e. you are able to find shares to short or your broker allows you to short the particular stock) this can be a lucrative strategy. The key to this strategy is to short into the price spike on the announcement day (preferably when the shares go "parabolic"). Based on experience, the shares will typically sell off within a week as mentioned – if they don't sell off, it is recommended to cover your position regardless (i.e. buy back the borrowed shares) to limit your risk (from potential continued increases in the share price and/or unforeseen take-over of the company).

6.4.3 Long-Term Stock Accumulation

Of course you can simply buy the shares of the company over time. This basic strategy works best when the company has several Phase II candidates near completion (i.e. next up, Phase III). If the company manages to move the Phase II candidates to Phase III, it will generally bring in new buyers and hence lift the share price. The key issue with this strategy is with regards to share price volatility if you decide to buy and hold. Your P&L will continuously fluctuate between losses and gains. As such, it is often a good strategy to trade around the position based on technical factors – this will allow you to capture some gains while you hold the position (which could be quite a long time). Another good strategy is to continuously sell Calls against the share (if available) thus bringing in a constant flow of income.

6.5 TRADE STRUCTURES NOT RECOMMENDED

There are several trade structures that are not recommended within the context of a major, late stage catalyst event. I discuss these structures in brief below.

6.5.1 Naked Put / Call Sale (at certain prices)

Selling Puts and Calls is, in theory, very lucrative in late stage biotech catalyst events given the high level of volatility (and hence the high premium value). However, there lurks a high level of danger when selling Puts or Calls at certain strike levels and with certain company/drug-specific fundamentals. Put and Call selling requires a deeper level of due diligence with regards to the fundamentals of the company and/or market potential of the drug candidate.

Ideally, Puts should only be sold for lower strikes (for example, strikes below $5 ~ $7.5) and for companies with stronger relative fundamentals. Make no mistake, a failed catalyst can result in a stock price decline of greater than 50% (and often greater than 75%) and often surpasses the value of the premium collected on the sale – the lower the strike, the lower the absolute potential loss.

For example, XYZ stock is trading at $10 three weeks prior to a Phase III catalyst. The 7.5 strike Put is trading at 1.70. You sell 10 7.5 strike Put @ 1.70 ($1,700 Credit). You make money as long as the stock does not drop beyond $5.80 (7.5 strike – 1.70 premium = $5.80), a 42% drop in the share price, not far out of the realm of possibility. If you engage in Put selling, be certain that the company has sufficient cash, other products in its pipeline, strong industry support, sources for future funding not associated with the late stage drug candidate, amongst other elements, for example, as you can eventually be assigned the shares. If you are assigned the shares (on a failed trial where the share price drops below the Put strike and you do not close out the position, i.e. you still like the prospects for the company), as mentioned, look to sell Calls against the stock position over the next several months as a way to recoup some of your losses. I would generally not recommend selling naked Calls as you may be caught off guard with an explosive (and unexpected) upward move in the shares due to spectacular results coupled with massive short covering and other elements. You could also be blind-sided by an unexpected acquisition of the company. The unbounded nature of naked Call selling makes it far too risky to use (in my opinion).

6.5.2 Straight Put / Call Buy

Following a major FDA or clinical trial catalyst, volatility will collapse – this is a certainty. As a review, the higher the implied volatility, the higher the option premium. **When buying a Call or a Put with high implied volatility, you need to be certain that the underlying share price movement (Delta) will outpace the drop in option premium value from the collapse in implied volatility (Vega).** Those new to options (especially in trading biotech) are often shocked at the drop in value in the option even when the trade makes the move they want. The impact of implied volatility on option premium is often not noticed outside of biotech (for non-professional, retail traders) because implied volatility does not usually get above 150% for companies in other sectors. As such, buying Calls or Puts as a stand-alone strategy **(just prior to a catalyst event)** is often a losing proposition without *massive and unexpected* stock price movement in either direction.

For example, stock XYZ is trading at $5.00 a few weeks prior to a Phase III announcement. You are bullish on the company and buy 100 7.5 strike Call for 1.00 ($10,000 Debit) with implied volatility at 385%. The announcement is positive and the stock trades to $8.00. Due to the announcement (the news is out, uncertainty is gone), implied volatility collapses *immediately* to 85% and the Call option your bought now trades at 0.85 resulting in a $1,500 *loss*. Despite the huge $3 gain in the stock and the fact that the shares trade well above the 7.5 strike, the collapse in implied volatility outpaces the Delta gain on the shares, as such, you lose. In this situation, you should probably seek to immediately close out the position as waiting will cause the options to lose even more value as expiration approaches (parabolic increase in Theta for this short term option) and as liquidity decreases with associated widening of the Bid / Ask spread (thus further increasing your loss).

The same situation holds for a Put buy. For example, stock ABC is trading at $4.00 a few weeks prior to a Phase III announcement. You are bearish on the name and the 2.5 strike Put looks "cheap" at 0.40. You buy 100 at 0.40 ($4,000 Debit) – (actually they are quite expensive at 380% Implied Volatility). The results are negative and ABC stock price plummets to $2.00. Your Puts increase to 0.50 (implied volatility drops to 90%). You show a small profit but there is a problem – you need to get out of the position – this will be difficult as any profit you show will be eaten away by the Bid / Ask spread. If you decide to wait, the Bid / Ask will get wider and you risk having a losing position as shorts cover their positions (i.e. those who where short the stock buy the shares back) over the ensuing days and the stock shows some price increases. For you to make money on these types of trades, you need the shares to get absolutely slaughtered – in some cases, this strategy may work (i.e. where the company has no cash, one Phase III (which just failed), and some debt, and no other prospects, amongst other poor fundamentals).

If you use Put or Call buying as a stand alone strategy, it is highly suggested to do so **well in advance of the catalyst event** when levels of implied volatility are significantly lower (i.e. the options are actually cheaper). Also, consider using a spread structure, as discussed – in such situations, the high levels of implied volatility you are buying are offset by the high levels of implied volatility you are selling.

6.5.3 Straddle / Strangle Buy

Straddle and Strangle buying are probably the single worst strategies to use when trading small cap biotech FDA or clinical trial catalyst events (again, applies when the catalyst event is near and when implied volatility is at its highest). This is because you are paying for extremely high levels of implied volatility. You need massive stock price moves in excess of what the market is pricing just to break even. The only time it makes some sense to use these structures is where and when implied volatility is low and the catalyst event is more than 3 to 6 months away.

6.5.4 Covered Call (above certain price)

As discussed in Section 6.11: Extreme Volatility Covered Call, the key risk for this structure is the potential downside move. In almost all negative outcome situations, the premium sold against the share position will be insufficient to cover the losses. As such, I would highly suggest this structure be avoided where the share price exceeds $7.50 (or in accordance with your own risk profile). Do your due diligence.

CHAPTER 7.0

TRADE PROCESS

7.1   OVERVIEW

In the situation where you don't have a bullish, a bearish or a neutral trade conviction, you may be confused as to what approach, if any, to adopt for a trade (if you have a strong conviction, by all means trade *that* conviction). In the context of trading FDA or clinical trial catalysts, the outcome can often appear random (even for highly knowledgeable industry experts) and thus nearly impossible to determine in advance which trade structure to use. Smart trading involves seeking out the best situation(s) where risk is minimized and reward is maximized – trading FDA and clinical trial catalysts is all about searching for and maximizing these *asymmetric* situations.[47]

7.2   DEVISING A TRADE: THE PROCESS

The most efficient way to approach a catalyst trade, where you have no initial conviction and where the intent is to maximize asymmetry in the position, is to follow a standardized analytical framework. The point of this exercise is to identify all of the relevant data points and to use them to identify and construct the optimal trade structure. In this section I outline a straightforward process to achieve this goal. In Section 7.3, several example trades are provided.

---

[47] In my opinion, if one assumes equal probabilities for a catalyst outcome (i.e. 50% positive outcome, 50% negative outcome), a strategy that maximizes asymmetry, should be expected to yield, on average, out-performance (i.e. high returns) – think about it.

7.2.1 Define Risk Capital & Risk Structure

It is important at the outset to determine not only how much you wish to risk on any given trade but also how the risk in the trade is structured (i.e. is it defined or is it undefined?). The amount of risk you wish to take is a personal decision – as such, you need to decide for yourself. I personally prefer to risk no more than 1~2% of total capital (on the aggressive side) with risk structure completely defined in the trade (that is, no naked positions with undefined risk). I may increase or decrease the amount of risk depending on the level of opportunity to generate outsized returns.

7.2.2 Establish Time, Value & Volatility Boundaries

Prior to structuring a trade it is important to first establish *the boundaries of the trade in terms of time, value (i.e. stock price) and volatility.* You want to know (1) when (or around when) the catalyst will take place (2) where the stock will trade on either a positive or negative outcome and (3) the levels of implied volatility. This exercise, and its outputs, is basically the summation of all the elements of your analysis.

(1) Time

First, determine the timing of the catalyst and whether it is specific or estimated. FDA related catalysts are usually specific (such as PDUFA or Advisory Panels) and clinical trial related catalysts are usually estimated. Several points need to be made with respect to catalyst timing:

- Specific action dates can be changed – if this happens, implied volatility will collapse in the option series where the catalyst was originally expected (i.e. the options will lose substantial value) – the only hedge against this possibility (if you are long) is to either reduce your position size (if there is doubt) or to trade the following series.

- For specific catalysts, be careful when structuring a trade where the specified date is close to an option expiration date. For example, although PDUFA dates are specific, there may be a slight delay when the result is actually made public – nothing is worse than having made the right trade but having it expire prior to the actual catalyst. One can avoid this by either trading the next available series or by choosing, in advance, a time to exit the current series and roll into the subsequent series.

- The less specific an estimated catalyst date (such as "sometime in the 3rd quarter"), the less amount of capital one should risk. Don't forget that the eventual catalyst could fall well beyond the expiration of your option position.

(2) Value

Next, determine the bounds of the stock price for a negative or a positive outcome. This is achieved, as discussed, by analyzing company (and product) fundamentals, price on failure, analyst price estimates[48], option implied prices and prior technical levels (amongst other methods)[49] – these topics were already discussed in prior sections of this book.[50] Identified valuation benchmarks need to be aggregated to determine (approximately) where the stock may trade for both a negative and positive catalyst outcome.

(3) Volatility

Finally, determine where "current" implied volatility is relative to "normal" implied volatility (i.e. levels where there is no catalyst). This is achieved by

---

[48] Analyst estimates can be sourced from your broker, Twitter or other news media.

[49] Other methods include, for example, discounted cash flow (DCF) valuation. This valuation method was not covered in this book.

[50] See Chapter 3 (company fundamentals), Section 5.15 (price on failure), Section 5.7 (option implied prices) and Section 3.6 (prior technical levels).

comparing historic and current levels of implied volatility.[51] In most situations, the closer the catalyst date, the higher the level of implied volatility. Several points need to be made with respect to implied volatility:

- When structuring trades make sure to also take a look at the other option series around the catalyst series. For example, if a clinical trial result is estimated to take place in the SEP series, one should also pay attention (at the very least) to the OCT series when planning a trade. As discussed, big discrepancies in implied volatility between two series often yields interesting trading opportunities.

- For catalysts that are several months out, don't forget to include in your trade assessment the potential to profit from the increase in implied volatility (i.e. don't just focus on the "run up" in the share price). One can profit handsomely if only from the increase in implied volatility on into the catalyst date.

7.2.3 Determine Logic Based Conviction

If you have determined the time, value and volatility boundaries, you can begin to piece together potential trade structures with decent asymmetric characteristics – again, this is the route to take where you have no trade conviction or bias. In this step (many of whom consider obvious), consider what is logical or "what makes the most sense" given the time, value and volatility boundary data points. Here are a few examples of the thought process involved:

- A long (bullish) strategy may be more appropriate for a low priced stock with low implied volatility and a major late stage catalyst six months away – it would not make sense, at this juncture, to trade this from the short

---

[51] See Section 5.8 and Section 4.4.1.

(bearish) side. Perhaps a leveraged Call, outright Call purchase, a Call spread or Put sale is appropriate.

- A short (bearish) strategy may be more appropriate for a stock that has already exceeded analyst (upside) price targets several days prior to a PDUFA with high implied volatility – it would not make sense, at this juncture, to trade this from the long (bullish) side. Perhaps a Put spread, straddle sale, low cost/no cost butterfly or box structure is appropriate.

This goal of this step is to basically (and actively) engage in a non-biased, no holds bared, look at what trade conviction (i.e. bullish, bearish or neutral) appears to be the most logical and what trade structures to potentially employ – the more possibilities considered, the greater chance at discovering "the top" asymmetric position for the catalyst.

7.2.4 Option Chain Scan

You have determined your risk, you know the time, value and volatility boundaries and you have determined the logical trade conviction – the next and final step (aside from execution) involves actively seeking out and pricing the structures from the option chains. This is where you determine which structure has the maximum asymmetric profile (i.e. the structure with the lowest risk and the highest return). Several points need to be made with respect to scanning the option chain:

- Again, consider all possibilities (different strikes, Puts, Calls, different series, etc.) – you may be surprised at what you find.
- Never trade at the Bid or Ask – always assume that you can get a better price than the market is quoting.[52] The price the market is quoting is a price truly for suckers.

---

[52] See Section 5.6.

- Be aware of the risks when you decide to leg into a trade.[53]

- Never rush a trade – some trades take multiple days to fill. Let the market come to your desired level. It is better to miss a trade than to rush it and be filled at a bad price.

- Trade strategically – always consider your next move after you initiate your position (to enhance asymmetry). For example, if you buy a Call and the shares run, consider selling a higher strike Call. If the shares then appear to be stuck in a range, consider transforming the Call spread into a butterfly. Trading strategically is all about the continued (real time) evaluation of your position with the goal of lowering risk while increasing profit.

---

[53] See Section 5.4.

7.3 EXAMPLE TRADES

7.3.1 Trade #1

Background

XYZ Pharmaceuticals (XYZ) is expecting to receive a response from the FDA on Wednesday, March 16 whether or not their drug candidate is approved (five days away) – this is a PDUFA catalyst with a specific date. The response from the FDA is not expected to experience a delay. XYZ stock price has run up from around $3.00 a share to $10.00 a share on expectations that the drug candidate will be approved. According to the aggregated value data, the shares should trade around $10.00 to $13.00 on approval and around $7.00 on a "soft"[54] CRL (and around $1.50 for a "hard" CRL). Implied volatility is currently around +300% versus normal implied volatility of 90% – Put implied volatility is noticeably lower than Call implied volatility. Risk for this trade is set between $1,000 and $3,000.

Exhibit 7.1: Trade #1 Boundary Data

Boundary	Comment
Time	March 16 *(no delay expected)*
Value:	(-) = $7.00 (< $1.50 on hard CRL)
	(+) = $10.00 ~ $13.00
Fundamental	(-) limited pipeline, high cash burn
	(+) strong ownership
Price on failure	< $1.50 (extreme case)
Option implied	Range $7.00 - $13.00
Analyst estimates	High $12.50 / Low $10.00
Prior technical levels	N/A *(no prior PDUFA for drug)*
Implied Volatility	+300% (versus 90% "normal")

Conviction

XYZ shares have already increased to the value zone (it can be argued that the shares are nearly fully valued). The stock currently trades at or near most

---

[54] A "soft" Complete Response Letter (CRL) is one that can be rectified in the near to medium term whereas a "hard" CRL can only be rectified in the long term (i.e. requiring expensive new trials, etc.).

analyst price estimates. Options are currently implying a $3.00 move in either direction placing the shares to $13.00 on positive news and $7.00 on negative news. There is a discrepancy between Call (higher) and Put (lower) implied volatility (which is surprising given the company's low cash balances, high cash burn and limited pipeline) – clearly the market is expecting approval.[55] **Conclusion:** The drug will (likely) be approved but the shares will only experience a limited rise and most likely a decline because the company needs to raise cash (and will likely do so via a secondary offering soon after approval) – a conservative bearish strategy targeting a limited (no more than $1.00) decline is thus suggested. **Potential strategies to consider:** Long Put Spreads, No Cost/Low Cost Put Butterfly, Straddle Sale. **Outlier strategy:** (for extreme downside move) Long Put Spread.

Exhibit 7.2: Trade #1 Boundary Diagram

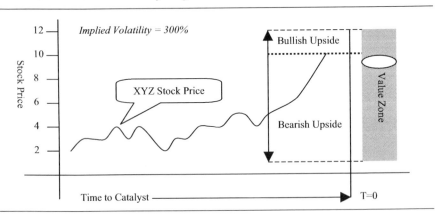

---

[55] This text is meant to highlight a summary thought process – obviously one would not base an entire trade on only this element.

163

Option Chain Scan

Next we check the MAR option chains for XYZ stock in Exhibit 7.3 and scan and price the potential identified strategies.

Exhibit 7.3: Option Chain for XYZ Stock

Stock: XYZ @ $10.00
Today: Wednesday, March 11
SERIES: MARCH

CALLS					PUTS			
BID	ASK	Volume	O.I.	STRIKE	BID	ASK	Volume	O.I.
				MAR 2.0	0.00	0.05		
				MAR 4.0	0.10	0.15		
				MAR 7.0	0.30	0.35		
				MAR 8.0	0.45	0.50		
				MAR 9.0	0.85	0.95		
1.55	1.65			MAR 10.0	1.35	1.45		
				MAR 12.0				

Here are the results of the scan and pricing exercise:[56]

Put Spreads:

#1	*Buy 20 MAR 10.0 strike Put, Sell 20 MAR 8.0 strike Put for 0.95 Debit*
	P&L: $1,900 Debit (=0.95 x 20 x 100)
	Max Risk/Reward: $1,900 / $2,100
#2	*Buy 30 MAR 9.0 strike Put, Sell 30 MAR 7.0 strike Put for 0.60 Debit*
	P&L: $1,800 Debit (=0.60 x 30 x 100)
	Max Risk/Reward: $1,800 / $4,200
#3	*Buy 100 MAR 4.0 strike Put, Sell 100 MAR 2.0 strike Put for 0.10 Debit*
	P&L: $1,000 Debit (=0.10 x 100 x 100)
	Max Risk/Reward: $1,000 / $19,000 (this is the "outlier" trade)

---

[56] Again, it should be possible to trade inside the Bid / Ask – hence pricing amounts shown in the examples will be better than market quotes.

Straddle Sale:

#1	*Sell 10 MAR 10.0 strike Call, Sell 10 MAR 10.0 strike Put for 2.95 Credit*
	P&L: $2,950 Credit (=2.95 x 10 x 100)
	Max Risk/Reward: $5,550[57]/ $2,950 (where stock trades @ $10 on exp.)

Low Cost / No Cost Butterfly:

#1	*Buy 100 MAR 10.0 strike Put, Sell 200 MAR 9.0 strike Put, Buy 100 MAR*
	8.0 strike Put for 0.15 Debit
	P&L: $1,500 Debit (=0.15 x 100 x 100)
	Max Risk/Reward: $1,500 / ~$8,400 (at $9.00)

Conclusion

Based on the characteristics of the identified trades, the best structures appear to be the Straddle Sale and the Low Cost / No Cost Butterfly. The issue with the Straddle Sale is the potential for very large losses should the company receive a hard CRL. The company has minimal cash and a limited pipeline – a hard CRL would be devastating to the company. Despite the unlikelihood of this occurring (based on market sentiment), I would give serious thought prior to using this structure. The issue with the Butterfly structure is the narrow profit zone (only makes money between $8.00 and $10.00; actually, this is the zone we expect). Another (major) issue with this structure is getting such a large order executed – in order for this trade to work, the options would need to be extremely liquid and it would likely take several days (if not over a week) to fill. Based on all the factors given, the best structure to use in this situation is most likely the No Cost / Low Cost Butterfly.

---

[57] Worst case scenario where stock trades to $1.50.

7.3.2 Trade #2

Background

ABC Biosciences (ABC) is slated to report top-line data for one of their Phase 3 drug candidates in "early to mid-March" (one month away) – this is a clinical trial catalyst with a vague estimated date. ABC share price has traded in a volatile range between $5.00 and $10.00 a share – the shares are currently at $9.00. According to the aggregated value data, the shares should trade around $12.00 to $15.00 on positive data and between $3.00 and $6.00 on negative data. Implied volatility is ~300% for MAR and ~200% for APR versus a normal implied volatility of 110%. Risk for this trade is set between $1,000 ~ $2,000.

Exhibit 7.4: Trade #2 Boundary Data

Boundary	Comment
Time	"early to mid-March" *(estimated)*
Value:	(-) = $3.00 ~ $6.00
	(+) = $12.00 ~ $15.00
Fundamental	(-) no approved drugs
	(+) strong pipeline, good cash balance
Price on failure	$3 *(part cash, part pipeline value)*
Option implied	Range $6.00 - $12.00
Analyst estimates	High $15.00 / Low $12.00
Prior technical levels	N/A
Implied Volatility	MAR ~300% (versus 110% "normal")
	APR ~200%

Conviction

ABC shares are currently trading in a mid-range between both downside and upside value estimates – neither bulls nor bears are in charge. The vague time estimate for release of top-line data (i.e. early to mid-March) has created a (very) large discrepancy in implied volatility between MAR and APR option series – apparently the market is placing more emphasis on the "early" language in the company statement thus implying the data will be released prior to MAR expiration (there remains a high risk, however, that the catalyst occurs *after* MAR expiration hence caution should be exercised when considering any MAR only strategy). ABC possesses excellent fundamentals including a solid pipeline and strong cash balances – this should support the share price on negative results thus potentially ruling out an outsized moved to the downside. **Conclusion:** A bullish strategy[58] that exploits the large implied volatility discrepancies between MAR and APR option series is suggested. **Potential strategies to consider:** "Split Month" Call Spread, Hedged Time Spread.

Exhibit 7.5: Trade #2 Boundary Diagram

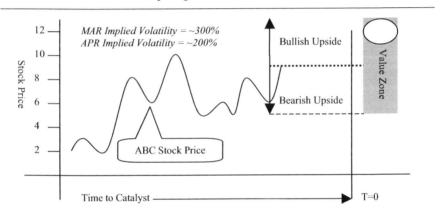

---

[58] Of course bearish trade structures would be explored in a real life trading situation – only the bullish is explored here for the purpose of brevity.

Option Chain Scan

Next we check the MAR and APR option chains for ABC stock in Exhibit 7.6 and scan and price the potential identified strategies.

Exhibit 7.6: Option Chain for ABC Stock

Stock: ABC @ $9.00
Today: Tuesday, February 1
SERIES: MARCH & APRIL

	CALLS				PUTS			
BID	ASK	Volume	O.I.	STRIKE	BID	ASK	Volume	O.I.
				MAR 3.0	0.15	0.30		
				MAR 4.0	0.45	0.60		
2.00	2.10			MAR 12.0				
1.80	1.90			MAR 13.0				
2.15	2.20			APR 12.0				
1.90	1.95			APR 13.0				

Here are the results of the scan and pricing exercise:

"Split Month" Call Spread:

#1	*Buy 50 APR 12.0 strike Call, Sell 50 MAR 13.0 strike Call for 0.35 Debit*
	P&L: $1,750 Debit (=0.35 x 50 x 100)
	Max Risk/Reward: $1,750 / $3,250[59]

Hedged Time Spread:

#1	*Sell 50 MAR 12.0 strike Call, Buy 50 APR 12.0 strike Call, Sell 50 MAR*
	3.0 strike Put for 0.05 Credit
	P&L: $250 Credit (=0.05 x 50 x 100)
	Max Risk/Reward: losses incur < $3.00 / $250 or profits +$12[60]

---

[59] It is important to note that if the shares trade above $13.00 by MAR expiration, this position will be assigned *short* shares. You can keep the short position or close out the entire trade.

[60] $250 profit if ABC > $12.00 before MAR expiration; after MAR expiration, profits occur above $12.00 (and can be quite substantial).

Hedged Time Spread (Continued):

#2	*Sell 20 MAR 12.0 strike Call, Buy 20 APR 12.0 strike Call, Sell 20 MAR 4.0 strike Put for 0.35 Credit* *P&L: $700 Credit (=0.35 x 20 x 100)* *Max Risk/Reward: losses incur < $4.00 / $700 or profits +$12.00*

Conclusion

Based on the characteristics of the identified trades, the best structure appears to be the Hedged Time Spread (with the sold MAR 3.0 strike Put). The fundamental strength of ABC provides some comfort with regards to selling the MAR 3.0 strike Put (in addition the worst case scenario downside price target is $3.00, right at the strike price – hence ABC would need to drop below the worst case estimate to begin to incur any losses). On positive news (and pre-MAR expiration), the trade only makes $250 – nothing to get excited about. However, if the news comes after MAR expiration, and the data is positive, our upside can be quite substantial (again, that is assuming we hold into data – once the MAR options expire, APR implied volatility will jump substantially thus providing a decent profit in its own right and an opportunity to simply sell the APR 12.0 strike Calls). If the position is not exited, a follow-on strategy in this scenario (i.e. after MAR expiration and pre-data), as discussed, would be to sell a higher strike APR Call against the existing APR 12.0 strike Call position to bring in even more premium and further enhance the profitability (and reduce risk) of the structure.

DRUG TRIAL & FDA GLOSSARY[61]

ABBREVIATED NEW DRUG APPLICATION ("ANDA"): An Abbreviated New Drug Application contains data that, when submitted to FDA's Center for Drug Evaluation and Research, Office of Generic Drugs, provides for the review and ultimate approval of a generic drug product. Generic drug applications are called "abbreviated" because they are generally not required to include preclinical (animal) and clinical (human) data to establish safety and effectiveness. Instead, a generic applicant must scientifically demonstrate that its product is bioequivalent (i.e., performs in the same manner as the innovator drug). Once approved, an applicant may manufacture and market the generic drug product.

ACTIVE INGREDIENT: An active ingredient is any component that provides pharmacological activity or other direct effect in the diagnosis, cure, mitigation, treatment, or prevention of disease, or to affect the structure or any function of the body of man or animals.

ADVERSE REACTION: An unwanted effect caused by the administration of drugs. Onset may be sudden or develop over time (See "Side Effects").

APPLICATION: See New Drug Application ("NDA"), Abbreviated New Drug

---

[61] AIDSinfo: Glossary of HIV/AIDS-Related terms 4th Edition, CenterWatch, Inc. Patient Resources: Glossary, ECRI (formerly the Emergency Care Research Institute), Eli Lilly and Company. Lilly Clinical Trials Glossary, MediStudy.com Inc. ClinicalTrials: A-Z Glossary, National Cancer Institute. Cancer.gov Dictionary, FDA.gov.

Application ("ANDA"), or Biologic License Application ("BLA").

APPLICATION NUMBER: See "FDA Application Number."

APPROVAL HISTORY: The approval history is a chronological list of all FDA actions involving one drug product having a particular FDA Application number. There are over 50 kinds of approval actions including changes in the labeling, a new route of administration, and a new patient population for a drug product.

APPROVAL LETTER: An official communication from FDA to a new drug application ("NDA") sponsor that allows the commercial marketing of the product.

APPROVED DRUGS: In the U.S., the Food and Drug Administration ("FDA") must approve a substance as a drug before it can be marketed. The approval process involves several steps including pre-clinical laboratory and animal studies, clinical trials for safety and efficacy, filing of a New Drug Application by the manufacturer of the drug, FDA review of the application, and FDA approval/rejection of application.

ARM: Any of the treatment groups in a randomized trial. Most randomized trials have two "arms," but some have three "arms," or even more (See "Randomized Trial").

BASELINE: (1) Information gathered at the beginning of a study from which variations found in the study are measured (2) A known value or quantity with which an unknown is compared when measured or assessed (3) The initial time point in a clinical trial, just before a participant starts to receive the experimental treatment which is being tested. At this reference point, measurable values such as blood pressure are recorded. Safety and efficacy of a drug are often determined by monitoring changes from the baseline values.

BIAS: When a point of view prevents impartial judgment on issues relating to the subject of that point of view. In clinical studies, bias is controlled by blinding and randomization (See "Blind" and "Randomization").

BIOLOGIC LICENSE APPLICATION ("BLA"): Biological products are approved for marketing under the provisions of the Public Health Service ("PHS") Act. The Act requires a firm who manufactures a biologic for sale in interstate commerce to hold a license for the product. A biologics license application is a submission that contains specific information on the manufacturing processes, chemistry, pharmacology, clinical pharmacology and the medical affects of the biologic product. If the information provided meets FDA requirements, the application is approved and a license is issued allowing the firm to market the product.

BIOLOGIC PRODUCT: Biological products include a wide range of products such as vaccines, blood and blood components, allergenics, somatic cells, gene therapy, tissues, and recombinant therapeutic proteins. Biologics can be composed of sugars, proteins, or nucleic acids or complex combinations of these substances, or may be living entities such as cells and tissues. Biologics are isolated from a variety of natural sources — human, animal, or microorganism — and may be produced by biotechnology methods and other cutting-edge technologies. Gene-based and cellular biologics, for example, often are at the forefront of biomedical research, and may be used to treat a variety of medical conditions for which no other treatments are available.

BLIND: A randomized trial is "Blind" if the participant is not told which arm of the trial he is in. A clinical trial is "Blind" if participants are unaware of whether they are in the experimental or control arm of the study; also called masked. (See "Single Blind Study" and "Double Blind Study").

CLINICAL: Pertaining to or founded on observation and treatment of participants, as distinguished from theoretical or basic science.

CLINICAL ENDPOINT: See "Endpoint."

CLINICAL TRIAL: A clinical trial is a research study to answer specific questions about vaccines or new therapies or new ways of using known treatments. Clinical trials are used to determine whether new drugs or treatments are both safe and effective. Carefully conducted clinical trials are the fastest and safest way to find treatments that work in people. Trials are in four phases: Phase I tests a new drug or treatment in a small group; Phase II expands the study to a larger group of people; Phase III expands the study to an even larger group of people; and Phase IV takes place after the drug or treatment has been licensed and marketed. (See "Phase I", "Phase II", "Phase III", and "Phase IV" Trials).

COHORT: In epidemiology, a group of individuals with some characteristics in common.

COMPASSIONATE USE: A method of providing experimental therapeutics prior to final FDA approval for use in humans. This procedure is used with very sick individuals who have no other treatment options. Often, case-by-case approval must be obtained from the FDA for "compassionate use" of a drug or therapy.

CONTRAINDICATION: A specific circumstance when the use of certain treatments could be harmful.

CONTROL: A control is the nature of the intervention control.

CONTROL GROUP: The standard by which experimental observations are evaluated. In many clinical trials, one group of patients will be given an experimental drug or treatment, while the control group is given either a standard treatment for the illness or a placebo (See "Placebo" and "Standard Treatment").

CONTROLLED TRIALS: Control is a standard against which experimental observations may be evaluated. In clinical trials, one group of participants is given an experimental drug, while another group (i.e., the control group) is given either a standard treatment for the disease or a placebo.

DATA SAFETY AND MONITORING BOARD ("DSMB"): An independent committee, composed of community representatives and clinical research experts, that reviews data while a clinical trial is in progress to ensure that participants are not exposed to undue risk. A DSMB may recommend that a trial be stopped if there are safety concerns or if the trial objectives have been achieved.

DIAGNOSTIC TRIALS: Refers to trials that are conducted to find better tests or procedures for diagnosing a particular disease or condition. Diagnostic trials usually include people who have signs or symptoms of the disease or condition being studied.

DOSE-RANGING STUDY: A clinical trial in which two or more doses of an agent (such as a drug) are tested against each other to determine which dose works best and is least harmful.

DOUBLE-BLIND STUDY: A clinical trial design in which neither the participating individuals nor the study staff knows which participants are receiving the experimental drug and which are receiving a placebo (or another therapy). Double-blind trials are thought to produce objective results, since the expectations of the doctor and the participant about the experimental drug do not affect the outcome; also called double-masked study. See "Blinded Study", "Single-Blind Study", and "Placebo."

DOUBLE-MASKED STUDY: See "Double-Blind Study."

DRUG-DRUG INTERACTION: A modification of the effect of a drug when administered with another drug. The effect may be an increase or a decrease in the action of either substance, or it may be an adverse effect that is not normally associated with either drug.

DRUG PRODUCT: The finished dosage form that contains a drug substance, generally, but not necessarily in association with other active or inactive ingredients.

DSMB: See "Data Safety and Monitoring Board."

EFFICACY: The maximum ability of a drug or treatment to produce a result regardless of dosage. A drug passes efficacy trials if it is effective at the dose tested and against the illness for which it is prescribed. In the procedure mandated by the FDA, Phase II clinical trials gauge efficacy, and Phase III trials confirm it.

ELIGIBILITY CRITERIA: Summary criteria for participant selection; includes Inclusion and Exclusion criteria.

EMPIRICAL: Based on experimental data, not on a theory.

ENDPOINT: Overall outcome that the protocol is designed to evaluate. Common endpoints are severe toxicity, disease progression, or death.

EPIDEMIOLOGY: The branch of medical science that deals with the study of incidence and distribution and control of a disease in a population.

EXCLUSION/INCLUSION CRITERIA: See "Inclusion/Exclusion Criteria."

EXPANDED ACCESS: Refers to any of the FDA procedures, such as compassionate use, parallel track, and treatment IND that distribute experimental drugs to participants who are failing on currently available treatments for their condition and also are unable to participate in ongoing clinical trials.

EXPERIMENTAL DRUG: A drug that is not FDA licensed for use in humans, or as a treatment for a particular condition (See "Off-Label Use").

FDA: See "Food and Drug Administration."

FDA ACTION DATE: The action date tells when an FDA regulatory action, such as an original or supplemental approval, took place.

FDA APPLICATION NUMBER: This number, also known as the NDA number, is assigned by FDA staff to each application for approval to market a new drug in the United States. One drug can have more than one application number if it has different dosage forms or routes of administration.

FOOD AND DRUG ADMINISTRATION ("FDA"): The U.S. Department of Health and Human Services agency responsible for ensuring the safety and effectiveness of all drugs, biologics, vaccines, and medical devices.

GENERIC DRUG: A generic drug is the same as a brand name drug in dosage, safety, strength, how it is taken, quality, performance, and intended use. Before approving a generic drug product, FDA requires many rigorous tests and procedures to assure that the generic drug can be substituted for the brand name drug. The FDA bases evaluations of substitutability, or "therapeutic equivalence," of generic drugs on scientific evaluations. By law, a generic drug product must contain the identical amounts of the same active ingredient(s) as the brand name product. Drug products evaluated as "therapeutically equivalent" can be expected to have equal effect and no difference when substituted for the brand name product.

INCLUSION/EXCLUSION CRITERIA: The medical or social standards determining whether a person may or may not be allowed to enter a clinical trial. These criteria are based on such factors as age, gender, the type and stage of a disease, previous treatment history, and other medical conditions. It is important to note that inclusion and exclusion criteria are not used to reject people personally, but rather to identify appropriate participants and keep them safe.

IND: See "Investigational New Drug."

INSTITUTIONAL REVIEW BOARD ("IRB"): (1) A committee of physicians, statisticians, researchers, community advocates, and others that ensures that a clinical trial is ethical and that the rights of study participants are protected. All clinical trials in the U.S. must be approved by an IRB before they begin. (2) Every institution that conducts or supports biomedical or behavioral research involving human participants must, by federal regulation, have an IRB that initially approves and periodically reviews the research in order to protect the rights of human participants.

INTENT TO TREAT: Analysis of clinical trial results that includes all data from participants in the groups to which they were randomized (See "Randomization") even if they never received the treatment.

INTERVENTION NAME: The generic name of the precise intervention being studied.

INTERVENTIONS: Primary interventions being studied: types of interventions are Drug, Gene Transfer, Vaccine, Behavior, Device, or Procedure.

INVESTIGATIONAL NEW DRUG ("IND"): A new drug, antibiotic drug, or biological drug that is used in a clinical investigation. It also includes a biological product used in vitro for diagnostic purposes.

IRB: See "Institutional Review Board."

LABEL: The FDA approved label is the official description of a drug product which includes indication (what the drug is used for); who should take it; adverse events (side effects); instructions for uses in pregnancy, children, and other populations; and safety information for the patient. Labels are often found inside drug product packaging.

MASKED: The knowledge of intervention assignment. See "Blind."

NDA: (see "New Drug Application")

NEW DRUG APPLICATION ("NDA"): When the sponsor of a new drug believes that enough evidence on the drug's safety and effectiveness has been obtained to meet FDA's requirements for marketing approval, the sponsor submits to FDA a new drug application ("NDA"). The application must contain data from specific technical viewpoints for review, including chemistry, pharmacology, medical, biopharmaceutics, and statistics. If the NDA is approved, the product may be marketed in the United States. For internal tracking purposes, all NDA's are assigned an NDA number.

NDA NUMBER: This six-digit number is assigned by FDA staff to each application for approval to market a new drug in the United States. A drug can have more than one application number if it has different dosage forms or routes of administration.

NME: (see "New Molecular Entity")
NEW MOLECULAR ENTITY ("NME"): A New Molecular Entity is an active ingredient that has never before been marketed in the United States in any form.

OFF-LABEL USE: A drug prescribed for conditions other than those approved by the FDA.

OPEN-LABEL TRIAL: A clinical trial in which doctors and participants know which drug or vaccine is being administered.

ORPHAN DRUGS: An FDA category that refers to medications used to treat diseases and conditions that occur rarely. There is little financial incentive for the pharmaceutical industry to develop medications for these diseases or conditions. Orphan drug status, however, gives a manufacturer specific financial incentives to develop and provide such medications.

PEER REVIEW: Review of a clinical trial by experts chosen by the study sponsor. These experts review the trials for scientific merit, participant safety, and ethical considerations.

PHARMACOKINETICS: The processes (in a living organism) of absorption, distribution, metabolism, and excretion of a drug or vaccine.

PHASE I TRIALS: Initial studies to determine the metabolism and pharmacologic actions of drugs in humans, the side effects associated with increasing doses, and to gain early evidence of effectiveness; may include healthy participants and/or patients.

PHASE II TRIALS: Controlled clinical studies conducted to evaluate the effectiveness of the drug for a particular indication or indications in patients with the disease or condition under study and to determine the common short-term side effects and risks.

PHASE III TRIALS: Expanded controlled and uncontrolled trials after preliminary evidence suggesting effectiveness of the drug has been obtained, and are intended to gather additional information to evaluate the overall benefit-risk relationship of the drug and provide and adequate basis for physician labeling.

PHASE IV TRIALS: Post-marketing studies to delineate additional information including the drug's risks, benefits, and optimal use.

PLACEBO: A placebo is an inactive pill, liquid, or powder that has no treatment value. In clinical trials, experimental treatments are often compared with placebos to assess the treatment's effectiveness. (See "Placebo Controlled Study").

PLACEBO CONTROLLED STUDY: A method of investigation of drugs in which an inactive substance (the placebo) is given to one group of participants, while the drug being tested is given to another group. The results obtained in the two groups are then compared to see if the investigational treatment is more effective in treating the condition.

PLACEBO EFFECT: A physical or emotional change, occurring after a substance is taken or administered, that is not the result of any special property of the substance. The change may be beneficial, reflecting the expectations of the participant and, often, the expectations of the person giving the substance.

PRE-CLINICAL: Refers to the testing of experimental drugs in the test tube or in animals - the testing that occurs before trials in humans may be carried out.

PREVENTION TRIALS: Refers to trials to find better ways to prevent disease in people who have never had the disease or to prevent a disease from returning. These approaches may include medicines, vitamins, vaccines, minerals, or lifestyle changes.

PROTOCOL: A study plan on which all clinical trials are based. The plan is carefully designed to safeguard the health of the participants as well as answer specific research questions. A protocol describes what types of people may participate in the trial; the schedule of tests, procedures, medications, and dosages; and the length of the study. While in a clinical trial, participants following a protocol are seen regularly by the research staff to monitor their health and to determine the safety and effectiveness of their treatment (See "Inclusion/Exclusion Criteria").

RANDOMIZATION: A method based on chance by which study participants are assigned to a treatment group. Randomization minimizes the differences among groups by equally distributing people with particular characteristics among all the trial arms. The researchers do not know which treatment is better. From what is known at the time, any one of the treatments chosen could be of benefit to the participant (See "Arm").

RANDOMIZED TRIAL: A study in which participants are randomly (i.e., by chance) assigned to one of two or more treatment arms of a clinical trial. Occasionally placebos are utilized. (See "Arm" and "Placebo").

REFERENCE LISTED DRUG (see "RLD")

REVIEW: A review is the basis of FDA's decision to approve an application. It is a comprehensive analysis of clinical trial data and other information prepared by FDA drug application reviewers. A review is divided into sections on medical analysis, chemistry, clinical pharmacology, biopharmaceutics, pharmacology, statistics, and microbiology.

REVIEW CLASSIFICATION: The NDA and BLA classification system provides a way of describing drug applications upon initial receipt and throughout the review process and prioritizing their review.

REFERENCE LISTED DRUG ("RLD"): A Reference Listed Drug ("RLD") is an approved drug product to which new generic versions are compared to show that they are bioequivalent. A drug company seeking approval to market a generic equivalent must refer to the Reference Listed Drug in its Abbreviated New Drug Application ("ANDA"). By designating a single reference listed drug as the standard to which all generic versions must be shown to be bioequivalent, FDA hopes to avoid variations among generic drugs and their brand name counterpart.

RISK-BENEFIT RATIO: The risk to individual participants versus the potential benefits. The risk/benefit ratio may differ depending on the condition being treated.

SIDE EFFECTS: Any undesired actions or effects of a drug or treatment. Negative or adverse effects may include headache, nausea, hair loss, skin irritation, or other physical problems. Experimental drugs must be evaluated for both immediate and long-term side effects (See "Adverse Reaction").

SINGLE-BLIND STUDY: A study in which one party, either the investigator or participant, is unaware of what medication the participant is taking; also called single-masked study. (See "Blind" and "Double-Blind Study").

SINGLE-MASKED STUDY: See "Single-Blind Study."

STANDARD TREATMENT: A treatment currently in wide use and approved by the FDA, considered to be effective in the treatment of a specific disease or condition.

STANDARDS OF CARE: Treatment regimen or medical management based on state of the art participant care.

STATISTICAL SIGNIFICANCE: The probability that an event or difference occurred by chance alone. In clinical trials, the level of statistical significance depends on the number of participants studied and the observations made, as well as the magnitude of differences observed.

STUDY ENDPOINT: A primary or secondary outcome used to judge the effectiveness of a treatment.

STUDY TYPE: The primary investigative techniques used in an observational protocol; types are Purpose, Duration, Selection, and Timing.

SUPPLEMENT: A supplement is an application to allow a company to make changes in a product that already has an approved new drug application ("NDA"). CDER must approve all important NDA changes (in packaging or ingredients, for instance) to ensure the conditions originally set for the product are still met.

SUPPLEMENT NUMBER: A supplement number is associated with an existing FDA New Drug Application ("NDA") number. Companies are allowed to make changes to drugs or their labels after they have been approved. To change a label, market a new dosage or strength of a drug, or change the way it manufactures a drug, a company must submit a supplemental new drug application ("sNDA"). Each sNDA is assigned a number which is usually, but not always, sequential, starting with 001.

SUPPLEMENT TYPE: Companies are allowed to make changes to drugs or their labels after they have been approved. To change a label, market a new dosage or strength of a drug, or change the way it manufactures a drug, a company must submit a supplemental new drug application ("sNDA"). The supplement type refers to the kind of change that was approved by FDA. This includes changes in manufacturing, patient population, and formulation.

TENTATIVE APPROVAL: If a generic drug product is ready for approval before the expiration of any patents or exclusivities accorded to the reference listed drug product, FDA issues a tentative approval letter to the applicant. The tentative approval letter details the circumstances associated with the tentative approval. FDA delays final approval of the generic drug product until all patent or exclusivity issues have been resolved. A tentative approval does not allow the applicant to market the generic drug product.

THERAPEUTIC BIOLOGIC PRODUCT: A therapeutic biological product is a protein derived from living material (such as cells or tissues) used to treat or cure disease.

TOXICITY: An adverse effect produced by a drug that is detrimental to the participant's health. The level of toxicity associated with a drug will vary depending on the condition which the drug is used to treat.

TREATMENT IND: IND stands for Investigational New Drug application, which is part of the process to get approval from the FDA for marketing a new prescription drug in the U.S. It makes promising new drugs available to desperately ill participants as early in the drug development process as possible. Treatment INDs are made available to participants before general marketing begins, typically during Phase III studies. To be considered for a treatment IND a participant cannot be eligible to be in the definitive clinical trial.

TREATMENT TRIALS: Refers to trials which test new treatments, new combinations of drugs, or new approaches to surgery or radiation therapy.

INDEX

ABOUT THE AUTHOR

Tony Pelz was a trader on a major European bank's proprietary trading desk. He was responsible for a portfolio with limits of more than $200 million. Prior to proprietary trading, Mr. Pelz worked with several major global investment banks in roles ranging from corporate finance, mergers and acquisitions to credit and business development.

He has substantial international work experience in Asia, U.S., Europe and Latin America and was based in New York City, Bogotá (Colombia), Rio de Janeiro (Brazil) and Amsterdam (The Netherlands).

Mr. Pelz currently resides in Denver, Colorado where he trades for his own account. He is married and has a young son.

Made in the USA
Lexington, KY
16 September 2011